PENGUIN VEER

COMMANDED BY DESTINY

General Satyawant Mallannah Shrinagesh was an Indian military officer who served as Chief of Army Staff of the Indian Army from 1955 to 1957. General Shrinagesh retired on 7 May 1957, completing thirty-four years of distinguished military service. Post retirement, he served as the Governor of Assam (1959–62), Andhra Pradesh (1962–64) and Mysore (now Karnataka, 1964–65). He also served as principal of the Administrative Staff College of India in Hyderabad from 1957 to 1959.

ADVANCE PRAISE FOR THE BOOK

'A fascinating account of the life and times of General S.M. Shrinagesh that captures the heady post-Independence spirit of nationalism and the role of the Indian Army in securing our hard-won freedom. The smooth transition of the army from one that was almost exclusively commanded by British officers to being wholly led by Indian officers bears testimony to the highest professional standards that prevailed, forged through lessons learnt from the barren mountains of the North-West Frontier Province to the sweltering battlefields of Burma. It is providential that this manuscript has seen the light of day, else this slice of history would have been lost for ever. I wish I had read this book while in service and been able to draw from this wealth of experience.'

—**Gen. (Dr) M.M. Naravane (Retd),**
PVSM, AVSM, SM, VSM, PhD

'General Shrinagesh's contribution to modernizing the post-Independence Indian Army and bringing about significant stability in military organizations, structures and *dastoors* is immense. The book, in addition to being a historical account, is an inspiring read on one of India's greatest military leaders.'

—**Lt Gen. K.J.S. Dhillon (Retd), author of**
Kitne Ghazi Aaye, Kitne Ghazi Gaye

'Reading *Commanded by Destiny* was like sitting across from General Shrinagesh himself, listening to a life lived with uncommon purpose. One moment that stayed with me long after I put the book down was his chilling account of the Devon aircraft fire—his calmness even as the plane plunged, his quiet humour even in the face of near-certain death [is remarkable]. It's emblematic of the man he was: steady, self-effacing and deeply human. This is not just a memoir; it's a blueprint for leadership, integrity and courage in the service of a young and uncertain nation. A compelling and necessary addition to the canon of Indian military history.'

—**Shiv Aroor, journalist and co-author of *India's Most Fearless***

COMMANDED BY DESTINY

A General's Rise *from* Soldier *to* Statesman

GENERAL S.M. SHRINAGESH

FORMER CHIEF OF ARMY STAFF
OF THE INDIAN ARMY (1955–57)

PENGUIN
VEER
An imprint of Penguin Random House

PENGUIN VEER

Penguin Veer is an imprint of the Penguin Random House group of companies whose addresses can be found at global.penguinrandomhouse.com

Published by Penguin Random House India Pvt. Ltd
4th Floor, Capital Tower 1, MG Road,
Gurugram 122 002, Haryana, India

Penguin
Random House
India

Portions of the book first appeared in Brigadier Satish K. Issar's book, *General S.M. Shrinagesh: Soldier, Scholar, Statesman,* published by Vision Books in 2009

First published in Penguin Veer by Penguin Random House India 2025

10 9 8 7 6 5 4 3 2 1

This book is a memoir, which is being published posthumously and is an honest reproduction of the author's own account. The original transcript contained a few isolated missing words that had faded or rubbed off over time. The editors filled in these missing words as per their judgement and the context of the surrounding text, staying consistent in the overall meaning and import of the transcript. However, the reader must note that the statements and views expressed in this book are the author's own and the facts contained in this book are as reported by him, which have been verified to the extent possible. The publisher assumes no responsibility and is in no way liable for the same.

Please note that no part of this book may be used or reproduced in any manner for the purpose of training artificial intelligence technologies or systems.

ISBN 9780143464976

Typeset in Sabon LT Pro by MAP Systems, Bengaluru, India
Printed at Thomson Press India Ltd, New Delhi

www.penguin.co.in

MIX
Paper | Supporting
responsible forestry
FSC® C010615

To

My mother,
Ahalyabai Mallannah Shrinagesh

General Shrinagesh: A soldier, a strategist, a statesman

Contents

Foreword

Although I never had the chance to spend time with my grandfather, our bond exists not through shared moments but through the ideals that continue to shape my journey. His life was intricately tied to the fabric of the Indian military and governance. His journey from Cambridge to Sandhurst, from the battlefields of Burma to the heights of Zoji La, culminated in him becoming the Chief of the Army Staff, the principal of the Administrative Staff College of India, Hyderabad, and then the first-ever military officer to be appointed Governor of Assam, Andhra Pradesh and Mysore successively.

My grandfather's military career began among a generation of young Indian officers who trained under the colonial system but carried in their hearts a deep sense of patriotism and a vision for a self-governed military. Perhaps his most enduring contribution was his advocacy for the Indianization of the Indian Army. At the time of Independence, India inherited a military institution that had been designed to serve British interests—where the ethos and structure of the army remained deeply colonial. My grandfather believed that India needed a military that reflected its own traditions, values and strategic priorities. His vision was not just about replacing British officers with Indians; it was about fostering a sense of national pride and self-sufficiency. He was known for his fairness, his ability to take tough decisions and his commitment to the well-being of the soldiers under his command—qualities that made him not just a respected officer but a deeply admired one, who is still remembered today.

For the Indian Army, his legacy is a reminder of the institution's strength, adaptability and the pioneering spirit that continues to define it. For the common reader, it is an opportunity to gain a deeper appreciation of the history and evolution of our armed forces.

As you turn the pages of this book, I hope you take inspiration from his journey and pride in our armed forces and find renewed respect for the men and women who dedicate their lives to the service of our nation.

1 April 2025,   Gaurav Shrinagesh
Gurugram

Introduction

The de Havilland Devon was a small, twin-engine propeller aircraft and an ideal seven-seater executive plane. It was comfortable to travel in, easy to handle, and could land and take off in reasonably small fields, particularly those that were built during the war for the India–China–Burma Theatre. A number of them had been left to us as disposal equipment at the end of the war and were being used by the Indian Air Force for executive and VIP transport; and many army officers had been moved from place to place, particularly for conferences, in this handy and versatile craft. The Devon was an excellent executive aircraft, except for a slight shortcoming—it could not maintain height on one engine.

On 3 February 1952, five senior army officers and I were returning from a conference in Lucknow in one of these Devons. To my horror, while gazing out of the window, I saw flames coming out of the port engine. The engine was obviously on fire, and the plane would explode the moment the fire reached the fuel system. The intercommunication door between the passengers and the cockpit showed the pilot, Flight Lieutenant Biswas, attempting desperately to extinguish the fire, when suddenly, the plane flipped and plunged down to 4000 ft. As the pilot succeeded in regaining control, my eyes sprang back to the port engine. The engine had miraculously disappeared, leaving a gap without any trace of flames. By a stroke of good fortune, the engine had fallen out with its flames, without affecting the fuel tanks. Until the reaction of relief flooded through me, I had not realized how tense I had become; but my relief was short-lived, because the Devon, I remembered, could not maintain height on one engine, and it was dusk. It would be difficult to force-land without being able to see the ground and without the ability to manoeuvre from such a low level. Flt Lt Biswas skilfully managed to locate a freshly harvested field and belly-landed us almost in the dark.

We disembarked from the plane unscathed, apparently in order of precedence, and walked to the nearest village a couple of miles away. We obtained a lift from the village to the main Lucknow Road in the only means of conveyance available—a bullock cart. By this time it was quite late, and search parties had been sent out to locate the supposedly burning aircraft. En route, we met one of these parties from Lucknow in an ambulance and explained light-headedly to the medical officer incharge, that we were sorry we had no work for him.

We were invited to spend the night at the residence of the Area Commander, Major General B.S. Chimney. He was my colleague at Sandhurst and a good friend. He reconnoitred the area the next evening at the exact time of the accident and concluded that we had had a miraculous escape, not only because the plane had not exploded mid-air but also because the plane, after it had belly-landed, came to a halt just by the side of a deep well and only two yards short of a large tree. If the accident had occurred a few minutes later, it would have been too dark for the pilot to spot the harvested field below. When we reached Maj. Gen. Chimney's residence, Mrs Chimney asked me how we had managed to get out of the burning plane. 'In the same order as we went in,' I replied without thinking.

Meanwhile, the SOS from the pilot mid-air, together with the fall of the burning engine had given the impression that the aircraft had descended in flames. A message was conveyed accordingly to the people concerned in Delhi. My wife, who was expecting the party to dinner that night, began to get nervous when the aide-de-camp (ADC) failed to give her any news of the arrival of the aircraft; and when he tried (long after it was due) to suggest that the plane would be landing shortly, she said, 'Now tell me the truth, what has happened?' The ADC then confessed that the plane had caught fire mid-air soon after it had taken off. She took some time to get over the shock. Thereafter, she asked her brother, Brigadier R.K. Kochhar, to come to the house immediately. Intuition made her feel that there was still hope, and she waited patiently. Among others, General Cariappa, the Commander-in-Chief, and Bakshi Ghulam Mohammad, the deputy prime minister of Jammu and Kashmir, who was then visiting Delhi, called at the house. Gen. Cariappa explained that search parties had been sent to locate the plane and that no effort would be spared.

Around midnight, news came through that we were all safe, and my own telephone reached my wife. She could not believe that we had escaped unscathed or without being covered in bandages, so much so that despite assuring her that all was well, she said she would not speak to me if I were merely attempting to assuage her feelings, and if she found a single scratch on me.

Flt Lt Biswas was decorated with the Ashoka Chakra, Class I, by the President for his cool-headed and adroit handling of the plane in extremely difficult circumstances. Later, the prime minister, Shri Jawaharlal Nehru, wrote to me the following comments: 'As it is all over now, one can look back upon it with composure. It is perhaps a good thing to face such contingencies provided one survives.' It is an irony of fate that Flt Lt Biswas, who had saved us from almost certain destruction, had to lose his own life in an air crash about two years later.

As a result of this adventure, the Devons were used sparingly and were eventually replaced by other aircraft, which later became available for this task. Another outcome of this trip was that we agreed that our top personnel, though individually replaceable, were not replaceable in numbers. Thus, they were therefore not to travel together in one aircraft.

The six officers travelling in the aircraft were Thimayya, Thorat, Mohinder Singh Chopra, Sardanand Singh, Ajaib Singh and I. Gen. Thimayya, a typical Sandhurst product, was a fine soldier, almost flamboyant, respected and loved by his officers and men. He later succeeded me as the Chief of the Army Staff, soon after which Shri Krishna Menon took over as defence minister. He could not accept Mr Krishna Menon's attempts to control the detailed administration of the army. He was later selected as the chief mediator of the UN in Cyprus because of his flair and ability. He unfortunately died there in harness due to a heart attack. Gen. Thorat, another distinguished soldier, who was capable enough to succeed him later as Chief of the Army Staff, had perforce to leave the army because he supported his own chief's views during Shri Krishna Menon's tenure of office. He was later selected as chairman of the Bombay Public Service Commission. Gen. Sardanand Singh, who was later to be on my staff during the Kashmir operations, is now the top executive of a highly successful public-sector organization, Indian Oil. Gen. Chopra is heading a civil organization in physical education in Punjab, while Ajaib Singh, who retired as a brigadier, preferred farming in northern India. I wonder whether he has not been the wisest of us all. I, after retiring as Chief of the Army Staff, became the founder–principal of the Administrative Staff College at Hyderabad and later was fortunate enough to have experience as Governor. I have often wondered why these officers selected the army as their profession.

1
Early Days

What influences a young man to choose his particular career—his parents, his family, his education or upbringing or perhaps his environment? For me the choice of a profession was a very difficult one, because at the time when the army career was open to us, I was at Cambridge, having passed my 'Little Go', preparing for a career in civil life.

Cambridge has many attractions—its pleasant surroundings steeped in tradition, its academic atmosphere, its challenge of new ideas, its freedom of thought and action and its opportunity for exercising a choice in one's activities—curricular or extracurricular. In a soldier's profession, the stress would be on uniformity and discipline; there would be limitations on the exercise of one's own choice and one's own activity, and there might even be restrictions on freedom of thought and action. In a military career, there would be much more hardship as well, and of course, the periodical prospect of combat. I had been at a public school in England for several years, and discipline was not unfamiliar to me. In ordinary circumstances, life at Cambridge would appear to be more acceptable than the discipline at Sandhurst. Yet, a military career appealed to me.

My father Dr Shrinagesh Mallannah, a student of the renowned Professor Robert Koch of Germany, had established himself in Hyderabad as the foremost bacteriologist after a distinguished scholastic record at Edinburgh and Germany. He had also done extensive research in the field of plague and other diseases in India. Some of his research work had been appreciated and published in Germany in the early part of this century. He also became a consultant to His Excellency Highness (HEH) the Nizam of Hyderabad and had developed an extensive practice. My father was greatly respected because he was devoted to his profession, and the demand it made on him left him very little time. His dedication led to overwork and a stroke of paralysis, resulting in his death at the early age of fifty-seven.

My father had hoped that one of his children would follow his profession, and that this would enable him to pass on his knowledge and experience. One of my sisters (Malati) and my youngest brother (Madhukar) did, in fact, choose medical careers. But my father's illness during their early years prevented them from benefiting from his vast experience. My mother (who had been educated at Edinburgh), however, acquired a great deal of that medical experience, but she became responsible, on my father's death, to bring up by herself three young children (almost a second generation and all girls).

Before deciding to seek an entry into Sandhurst, I naturally consulted my father, who replied that he had left it to me—the choice of my profession. He aimed to give each of his children the very best education from early life and thereafter allow them to carve out their own careers as far removed from paternal influence as possible.

I also consulted my only relatives in England at that time, my maternal uncle and my youngest brother, Jayavant (known as J.M.). The latter had decided to enter Cambridge to prepare for a career, which he later adopted—the Indian Civil Service. He was most enthusiastic as he felt that a military career would be ideally suited to my temperament, saying, 'If there was a fight anywhere in the neighbourhood, you would be involved in it any way.'

My maternal uncle, Barrister Shamrao Kelavkar from Kolhapur, was an honest, upright man with strong nationalistic views. He had been in England throughout the First World War and admired those men in uniform with whom he had come in close contact. He felt that the armed forces represented one of the important social groups in any country and thought that the army was in my 'blood'. But he warned me that service with the armed forces would entail much sacrifice on my part and would not furnish a settled life of the civilian, because the soldier, even in peace, would have to serve in difficult, lonely, non-family stations with few amenities. Strongly nationalistic, he believed that Indians should serve in all walks of life and gain experience in all branches of the administration and services, as they would be of use to their country later when the country needed them.

What then influenced my decision? My own respect for the military profession had perhaps been formed by the fact that my grandfather had been a soldier and strengthened during my years at public school, and the fact that during most of those years, England was at war. Many of my contemporaries naturally joined the army then, and some of the most outstanding boys at school had selected the army as their careers and been through Sandhurst. Q.B. Callondar and M.R. Roberts had distinguished themselves in the war (both were lieutenant generals) and E.M. Bastyan, who was a prefect with me, also distinguished himself in a army career (he later became lieutenant general and ended his military career by becoming a Governor of an Australian state). Perhaps I rationalized my own hunch by thinking that in the coming years, the country would need men with military experience, and I could make some contribution. In those days, not long after the First World War, feelings of patriotism were thoroughly inculcated in boys at school, and I as one of them, longed to contribute to my homeland.

In pursuance of his aim to give the very best education to all of his children, my father sent my younger brother

(J.M.) and me to West Buckland, one of the public schools in England in Devon, at the very early ages of nine and eleven respectively. My youngest brother Madhukar followed; and years later, my second son Ashok continued the tradition.

I presume Ashok also went to West Buckland for his early schooling because of my desire and pride that he be associated with my old school. Looking back, however, I am not so certain that this was quite the best course from his point of view. In the first place, it is always best if each person gets to make his way through life (even at school) on his own and not based on the reputation of a relative—good or bad. Though Ashok became a prefect, appointed by a different headmaster—(a more difficult accomplishment than in my time because the number of boys was greater, so was the number of Indians who had passed through this school)—yet he suffered under the disability of being expected to emulate, if not better, the examples set by J.M., Madhukar and I. Apparently, we three brothers, who were closer in age, were often quoted as examples to Ashok. Because between the three of us, we had variously held the head prefectship of the school, captaincy of the school in cricket, football, shooting and athletics and head of the Officer's Training Corps (OTC) and scholarships to the university and entrance to Cambridge. Our name was on almost every honour board in the school, both for scholarship and for sport, including a second place in the cross-country run 'Exmoor'.

This run consisted of a walk of seven-and-a-half miles to the starting point and a run back on a steeple-chase course of nine miles, the last two of which were up very steep hills, while the first part of which was over the moors. I believe this is one of the toughest runs in the country, if not elsewhere, and it was lately televised by the BBC because of its length and difficulty. It was run at the end of the winter, whatever the weather; and I have taken part in it during a snowstorm when special arrangements had to be made over the nine-mile return course, to ensure that people on the route were not lost in the snow. Every member of the school over the age of twelve had to take part in it, I presume, because of the tradition of 'toughness', which the school had developed.

There was a further disadvantage in going to the same school, because this was neither a big public school, nor was it one of the well-known ones. Those people in the university or Sandhurst, who had been to large public schools, had a reputation preceding them already, particularly in sports. All, therefore, received recognition in the university team often in the first year, whereas my younger brother (J.M.) when he was asked for a 'trial' for the University Team for Rugby, had to inform the team's captain that he was not then eligible, being in his fourth year.

My father believed that the formative years should be spent under one system of education and during those formative years, children should not be exposed to more than one philosophy or social system, as that would undermine their sense of security and loosen their sociological anchorage. He, therefore, selected the school with great care; and after visiting a number of schools in England and Scotland, based his final decision principally on the ability and personality of the headmaster, Reverend Harries, a man of character and vision, with a flair for teaching, who had been in the educational line for many years. In those years, Mr Harries set the tone for most of the activities in the school, often taking part himself, in spite of his age, in a great number of them—in games, the dramatic society and other curricular and extra-curricular activities.

Mr Harries had a very straightforward approach and a thorough understanding of human nature, and he showed considerable courage during my last years at school in selecting an Indian (myself) as a prefect in an institution composed entirely of British boys, except for J.M. and I. In those days, prefects exercised considerable authority in extracurricular activities and in enforcing discipline, being permitted to enforce it by caning—though this was rarely resorted to. For them, caning did not seem to have the same sadistic overtones as attributed to it now.

As always, boys revelled in an attempt to do daring things without being caught. A common method was to read a novel during the hours set aside in the evening to prepare for the next day's work; though anyone with a novel would get so engrossed in it that he would be disciplined. One boy became a hero by naming periodically the prefect or master he was going to bait, irrespective of the consequences. He would, for example, stand at ease deliberately when a formal parade was called to attention, pretending that the words of command had not been heard even though they were repeated.

From amongst our masters, the greatest disciplinarian was Darvil, who had by then so established his reputation that he could take his teaching duties in a very relaxed manner. He used to teach us arithmetic and did so by the simple expedient 'of ordering us to get on with the next thirty sums' and promptly going to sleep. Woe be to him who had not 'got on with the next thirty sums' at the end of the period, or whenever he awoke. Perhaps one of the important influences in my school life, probably as much as Mr Harries, was Sam Howells, an unmarried housemaster, who had obviously studied and practised a great deal of psychology. He obtained a reputation for sixth sense in the third form. On one occasion, when he was walking away, he saw the reflection in the glass of a picture of a boy attempting to throw a dart, and still walking away from the boy without turning around, said quietly, 'Jones, come and see me afterwards'—a euphemistic form of announcing a punishment. On the other hand, boys in the sixth form felt that he respected their maturity, and he frequently had discussions with them. I felt very privileged and benefited from his conversations and advice during coffee and after-lunch sessions in his room.

The school itself, with its location on the edge of Exmoor, a wild hilly moor with a severe invigorating climate, gave me a sturdy constitution and excellent health. The training and the atmosphere at the school gave us self-reliance and the ability to fight our own battles. I was ragged for many years, about an incident when I was a new boy comparatively. I was at the swimming pool with a group of bigger boys, including the head prefect. I had just dived in when I heard the words 'duck him'. I apparently came up spluttering and demanded 'who said duck him?', preparing to take on anyone who had dared to make such a statement. There was an immediate explosion of mirth because it was the head prefect.

Perhaps as an important part of our development was the constant and regular inculcation of the value of group activity. The school encouraged only team games; golf and even tennis were frowned upon. Individual supremacy did receive its encouragement, but everything centred around the accomplishment of the group. The worst offence in the group was to let down the team. On occasion, the whole class was punished because someone had not owned up to a misdeed. No one let him down before the masters or the prefects, but all unitedly took it out of the miscreant later if they did not agree with him.

The group spirit, used to be almost an accepted code of conduct in most English public schools, and it has probably been developed in a few schools in India, notably schools like the Doon School, Mayo College, Lawrence School etc. We did not think much of the system, which prevented us from taking up seriously individual games like golf; nor did we appreciate fully at that time the value of working only for the team, which is said to be one of the characteristics that developed England into a great nation—that is the compulsion to fight for the side, for the team, or for the country and not just for one's self. This team spirit has been belittled, of late, also in England, where there has been a greater stress on individual development.

Maybe the stress on individual development is acceptable to an advanced country. But is there an advantage to be gained by a developing country in stressing teamwork, at a time when it is attempting to build a unified nation in the face of diverse influences and cultures? We have examples of brilliant men with outstanding individual performances but have often failed to take advantage of them in a team. The stick work of one of India's hockey forwards was a delight to watch when he dribbled the ball right through the opponent's combined opposition and from one end of the field to the other. But alas, he rarely created opportunities for a timely pass to a well-placed teammate to secure a winning goal. Have we not often seen the brilliance of a political leader's masterstrokes, but have resulted in the disruption of the organization? How often do regional interests in setting up industries or in other spheres take precedence over the needs of the country itself? How often has the regional language caused disruption of our essential unity? The philosophy of a socialist system and its organization is based on the development of a group and sometimes goes against the interest of the individual. Though we profess to be a socialistic society or aim to be one, we still prefer to act in a very individualistic manner. I am not enamoured by the complete domination of the state as in communist countries but often wonder if we should lay greater stress on working for the group or country, rather than for the individual.

Group pressures, it is known, are more difficult to withstand than pressures from ordinary controls, and the group is not always, logically or psychologically, sound in its actions. The use of the guillotine during the French Revolution is an example of the excesses in cold blood to which individuals can be driven to act in a group. The fantastic frenzy displayed on both sides of the border at the time of the Partition of the country is one of our sad experiences of group activity. I do not doubt that the Red Guards in China have also furnished other examples. Can we, however, as a developing nation, take advantage of the vast fund of individual talent and ability of our nationals, and utilize these talents for the advantage of the group or the country as a whole? Perhaps by building up a team tradition in India, either through schools or colleges or similar institutions, we might be able to infuse more unity in our joint economic, political and administrative endeavours.

While I was pondering on the various factors involved in choosing a profession, the career of an army officer had been thrown open to Indians. This added one more reason to my resolve to join the army, and I applied for admission to Sandhurst. The interview by the board still lingers in my memory. Walking along the long dark corridors of the War Office, though I was accompanied by my maternal uncle, seemed interminable. I entered the interview room alone, with some considerable trepidation and was faced by half a dozen distinguished formidable-looking Englishmen, of whom some were in military uniform. But their questions about my early education and my activities in school etc. soon put me at ease. My scholastic achievements, the fact that I was good at games, and that I had been selected as prefect and a sergeant in the OTC and was head of my house seemed to prepossess them in my favour. A month later, I was informed that I had been selected, and so I left Cambridge to report at Sandhurst (Royal Military College) at Camberley.

I have often wondered what I had missed in giving up life at Cambridge, which had a very different system of instruction to what we were accustomed to, almost a system of laissez-faire. The student at Cambridge was permitted, in consultation with his tutor, to select the areas of studies and the lectures he would attend, of course, covering a certain minimum number of hours—about ten to twelve a week. He was considered as fulfilling his attendance requirements, and his course, as long as his presence was noted at lectures, and provided he attended five dinners in his college hall each week.

It was difficult to avoid the five rather stereotyped dinners in the college hall, but there were many ingenious ways of avoiding lectures. Some professors marked attendance only at the commencement and the end of terms; some had so many students that they did not know them individually; others were interested only in the regular payment of fees. Freshmen soon discovered that the only essential requirement was to attend the five dinners each week.

Of course, there was an examination at the end of each year. And for the honours degree, the undergraduate was given only one chance. If he failed, he might be given a pass degree as consolation, but if he failed badly, he would never get another opportunity during his lifetime to sit for a Cambridge tripos. From the point of view of those coming directly from schools in India, this was a radical change from control to almost complete freedom. While I was there, one student had spent seven years in attempting to pass the Little Go, the entrance examination into Cambridge.

Cambridge has turned out many able Indian statesmen and administrators, also eminent professionals and businessmen; but equally many have fallen by the wayside for want of adequate guidance, or because their character formation had not been complete or because of the pull of other interests.

2

Sandhurst

Life at the Royal Military College (RMC), Sandhurst, was in many ways different from the life I was beginning to get accustomed to at Cambridge.

The Military College laid stress on implicit obedience to orders and precision in the execution of all tasks, however small. On the physical side, training included ceremonial parades where the emphasis was on drills of a very high standard. We were brought and kept up to the mark by sergeant instructors from the British Guards, who taught us to accept the exacting demands made on us by them, setting the highest standards.

For example, we were expected to stand rigidly at attention when speaking to our seniors, whether they were cadets or officers, addressing them as 'sir', even though there might only be a slight difference in seniority.

There was nothing subservient about this, as the drill instructors soon made us understand. A 'dressing down' always ended with a respectful (we hoped!) 'sir'. A hasty shave rarely went unnoticed and elicited the comment: 'You are looking unkempt this morning, sir.' The minute attention to detail and the rigid behaviour even in very small matters, though occasionally resented at that time, encouraged, I feel, mutual respect and taught discipline.

Of course, discipline had been misused, and there have been many excesses. Misuse has led to mutiny, as on the *HMS* Bounty, made famous by a film. More recently, a group of the US Marines marched into a swamp, under the strict discipline of a sergeant, resulting in seven of the leading ranks being engulfed and dying. US citizens are not such believers in discipline as those in Germany or Japan. Yet, they have been able to accept the necessity of such rigid discipline in the US Marines because they realized the value of it in conflict and the necessity for it during training. There are many good examples of the value of discipline presented in the course of history. There was an occasion when troops under a famous general became so incensed with certain grievances, that they decided to approach him 'en masse' almost in a state of mutiny.

Coming out of his tent, he called the heterogenous group to attention in his barrack-room voice and ordered 'about turn—quick march'. The troops reached their own lines in good order and did not again pick up sufficient courage to face him. In the meantime, the general quietly had the grievances removed. It was in Austerlitz that Napolean met his troops on a bridge, in a state of rout. Pointing in the direction of the enemy, he shouted, 'The enemy is there; advance', turning the rout into victory.

I have mentioned ceremonial parades purely as one of the methods of inculcating discipline, as it seemed clear to me that the British Army, which is also a servant of the state, had recognized that it was fundamentally a fighting weapon, mellowed by discipline out of a collection of individuals. To achieve discipline, it was an understandable necessity that orders should be implicitly obeyed. Discipline gives cohesion and strength, but most of all, it helps a group or a mass to conquer fear. In cold blood, very few men are prepared to die, and fear in a group or a mob can be a horribly terrifying thing. What induces a group in a battle to face death? Is it hope of fame or reward, or perhaps devotion to a cause or the country? Fame appeals to some; promotion and decoration mean something, but belief in a cause counts for much, if fostered by mass propaganda. Yet, there is truth in the saying that 'a man does not flee in battle because he is fighting for a righteous cause; he does not attack because his cause is just. He flees because he feels he is the weaker; he conquers because he is the stronger, or because, you and I, his leaders, have made him feel stronger'. Perhaps, of all the things that make a person strong in a group, the most important is disciplined behaviour.

On the academic side, the officer–instructors at Sandhurst were carefully selected from the British and Indian armies and were men of high calibre. Instruction on the military side was usually at the platoon level. Our company commander was a senior major who handled all instructions in the company and himself taught military history. His exposition of the Schlieffen Plan was brilliant, outlining in detail the moves of the German armies on the continent during the early phase of First World War and highlighting the German right-wing movement under (Alexander) von Kluck. Normally, however, officers who gave lectures were not assigned any other company duties, which gave them sufficient time to devote to the subject allotted to them and ensured a uniform standard of instruction. Tactics and military law were taught by selected infantry and cavalry officers, while frontier warfare was the responsibility of a senior officer of the army in India, who was also the guardian of the several Indian cadets at Sandhurst. General subjects were taught by officers of the Army Educational Corps, including English and scientific subjects. Cavalry officers conducted the riding courses, while weapons and drills were handled by sergeant instructors of the infantry and the guards.

Looking back, it appeared to me that the instructions in general were intended to teach and mould, rather than develop. Perhaps this was inevitable, as we were—apart from the British—quite a heterogeneous group; and it was necessary from the point of view of possible activity during war that we should be thoroughly indoctrinated with the idea of a disciplined group and be conversant with its evolution. Certainty, the teaching was neither on the lines of Gilbert (and Sullivan)'s 'Modern Major General', nor were we expected, for example, to know about Babylonian cuneiform, which perhaps was left for the Staff College. British officers appeared to have been so indoctrinated with the necessity for meticulous attention to detail that they invariably had very precise knowledge of their own units and often identified themselves very closely with them. An officer in a Sikh regiment, for example, was so conversant with Sikh traditions and identified himself so closely with their culture, that he might almost be accepted as a Sikh. Equally, officers of the other regiments turned themselves virtually into Tamilians or Punjabis etc. as the regiment required.

At the Royal Military College, there were two terms a year; and at the end of each term there were practical and written tests in all subjects, in which 'gentlemen cadets' had to reach the required standard if they were to continue at Sandhurst. The tests at the end of the fourth and final term, together with the ranks attained in the units, determined the order of passing out. Ranks of authority like corporal, sergeant and under officer carried many marks; but Indians, in my time, were not given these ranks. Rugby, football and cricket were considered more important games. As rugby was not generally played in India, no Indian found a place in the College Rugby Team. Cricket, hockey and tennis provided us with good opportunities to show our skills. For example, Gentleman Cadet Iskander Ali Mirza (who later became the President of Pakistan) won his Cricket Blues.

Individual ragging is present in every group, particularly in school and college, and Sandhurst was not an exception. It serves to teach the victim how to react and makes him a little less sensitive. But it can lead almost to tragedies in the case of nonconformists. In school, for example, it was soon discovered that a boy, Ellis, was afraid of water. From that moment, he had no peace on each occasion that he was near the water or near the swimming pool. He was reduced to hysteria by the ragging he received until it came to light there had been a drowning tragedy in his family. At Sandhurst, one of the cadets of my company was ragged so much that he became desperate, fixed his bayonet and charged a batch of British cadets in a narrow corridor. Fortunately, no one was seriously hurt; but the British cadets not only learnt to leave G.C. Balwant Singh alone but felt shy in future of all Indian gentlemen cadets.

The relationship between gentlemen cadets and officer–instructors was friendly but correct and distant. At some meals, officer–instructors sat at the same table with the cadets, but rarely did the company commander sit with us. In fact, I only saw our company commander closely once, when I was paraded before him on a charge of being frivolous at a ceremonial parade.

One early winter morning, I was in the front rank of my company, smartly turned out, for double, standing to attention with my rifle at my side. As I was the only Indian gentleman cadet, the long row of white hands, holding their respective rifles, was uniform, except for mine which broke the monotony. Unfortunately, I moved a little.

At that very moment, I heard a fierce shout from the opposite end of the square. 'You, there, sir, in No. 3 Company, the one wearing brown hand gloves . . .' This outburst had amused me, and I had just managed to suppress a laugh, but I was spotted. So, the next day I was paraded before my company commander and awarded the punishment of half a dozen extra drills on a charge of being frivolous on parade.

During the holidays, British cadets had their homes to go to, thus getting a break from the proximity of other gentlemen cadets and also some time in a family atmosphere. This break and the family atmosphere was what Indian cadets lacked because they could not contemplate a visit home during the holidays in those days, as air transport had been so little developed. Therefore, Indian cadets used to spend their holidays visiting parts of England, Great Britain or the European continent, in groups of their own.

I was little more fortunate, in that Mr Harries, my former headmaster, continued to be my guardian, and used to invite me to his home in North Devon. He had a wonderful family with three lovely boys, two of them identical twins; and his home was always full of guests. The twins were so alike in appearance that I believe their mother was the only one who could tell them apart. I have often wondered whether the extremely handsome twins ever adopted the tactics in reverse of the girl twins in Ian Hay's book. One of the girl twins there used to egg on a victim to the point of proposing marriage; whereupon the other would substitute and gently point out that he was perhaps mistaking her for her sister.

Of course, we thoroughly enjoyed the trips to the European continent. We were enticed by the weather in the Swiss or Italian lakes, or on the Riviera or entranced by the cafe life on the pavements. And I shall never forget the fabulous week we spent in Germany during their inflation, when our foreign money enabled us to live like 'lords' in the most palatial accommodation. But I welcomed the opportunity Devon afforded me to take part in cricket matches against the Somerset Stragglers or the Devonshire Dumplings, or even the leisurely day matches in the local village field. A local cricket match had its own appeal, with its lazy summer atmosphere, a leisurely day in the outfield, a chancy innings on an uncertain pitch, the good-humoured spectators, the strawberry tea and the gathering at the local pub.

All these relics of the past will not, unfortunately, reappear on the village scene in England again. Indian cadets at Sandhurst were few. During my time, there were not more than fifteen, as compared to some 700 British cadets, and very few had the advantage that I had of military training before joining Sandhurst. We realized that we had a long way to go before we could take our proper place with others. At the same time, we were made aware of the fact that we were unlike British cadets in many ways, and that we could not participate, con amore, in all their games and fun.

Conditions at school were different. Though my brother and I were the first Indians at the school, and there were others, we were rarely made to feel different from the rest of the school.

I suppose boys rarely consider differences of caste, colour or creed. In every activity, we took an active part and were included without question; and we made some very firm and lasting friends. My brother and I sometimes spent holidays at the homes of our respective friends—a compliment which we could not reciprocate. Of course, associating with one's own brother at school was simply not 'done'. But, at Sandhurst, the atmosphere was subtly different, and it took me a little time to realize it. British cadets were outwardly correct in their behaviour, but always distant and confined to their own circles.

Even those who were with me at school and close to me, gradually became more distant, and soon, quite aloof. Naturally, I wondered about the difference and the reason for it. Perhaps, it was the process of 'growing up' and coming to know the facets of life as they then existed for a colonial people. Perhaps, the atmosphere was partly set by the authorities who ran the college. If the latter, it was a mistake in the long run, because it raised in all of us that sense of resentment which not only welded our heterogenous group into 'Indians', but sparked the flame of intense 'patriotism' and made a number of us wish to prove that we were as good, if not better, at the activities, subjects or sports in which we were involved. I have mentioned Iskander Mirza's Blue. I, on the other hand, became determined to compete for the Quetta Cup, the cup awarded to the best man at arms passing into the Indian Army. The competition included outdoor subjects such as rifle and revolver shooting, riding, command on the square and similar activities designed for developing leadership qualities.

Possibly, therefore, Sandhurst developed in us that intense patriotism which characterized each one of us gentlemen cadets, who went through that regime, and that intense feeling continued throughout our lives. Symptoms of it appeared in Sandhurst when some of us wore *pagrees* instead of caps or played Indian music in the Mess.

Life at the RMC was exacting, and we were kept intensively busy from period to period, with little time to ourselves, to read, write or indulge in any form of relaxation. From the time we were woken by 'reveille' on bugles, to the evenings in the Mess, we were expected to be meticulous and scrupulously clean, and on parades, spotlessly turned out, in shining buttons, and highly polished Sam Browne belts and boots. Our main relaxation came on Sundays, when we were excused from attending chapel, got up late and usually gathered in the room of an Indian friend. On Saturday and Sunday nights, we were allowed passes to leave the college to go to London, where we often saw a play, and when we could afford it, dine at a fashionable restaurant. One Saturday, four of us decided to take out for the evening the topmost actress of the best show in town. We duly attended the theatre, went behind the stage after the show and met her in her dressing room, and I think impressed her with our joint admiration of her looks and talent. But, being new at the game, none of us plucked up enough courage to say that we four cadets wished to take England's top actress to supper. So, we came away with only the memory of a very brief half hour with a very gracious and charming person.

3

The Young Subaltern

I had done well at Sandhurst and had won the coveted Quetta Cup, awarded to the best man at arms (British or Indian) entering the Indian Army, and now I was to be posted to a regiment in India.

Up to that time, it was customary for officers passing out of Sandhurst and going into the Indian Army, to be posted for a year to a regiment wholly British in composition, stationed in India. This gave the officers a stipulated duration of orientation to India, time to learn about conditions on this subcontinent from their counterparts, as well as a period for their superiors to judge their temperamental suitability to the Indian Army. Those who finally opted out of India, or were found temperamentally unsuited, were either taken on the establishment of the British Army or permitted to terminate their services.

Was the same method of orientation to be used for Indians passing out of Sandhurst? Was any question of prestige involved? Characteristically, if any idea of British prestige was involved, it was overridden by the requirement of orientation and training. British regiments stationed in India were presumably good troops, adjusted to life in

India, and they would be in the best position to round off the training commenced at Sandhurst.

So, on arrival in India, we were all attached to British regiments, and I was fortunate enough to be posted to the 2nd Battalion, the North Staffordshire Regiment in Trimulgherry, which was near Hyderabad, where my parents (whom I had not seen for some time) were then.

There was also an advantage to us in being attached to a British regiment. Promotions in the British Army depended, amongst other factors, on vacancies in the regiment; and during peacetime, vacancies were few and far between. In the North Staffordshire Regiment, officers often served as much as eighteen years before they were promoted to captains. So, the Subalterns, with whom we were associated, were often mature men of experience, and we benefited a great deal from that association. In the Indian Army, promotions depended, among other matters, on a timescale, and not on vacancies in the regiment. In my time, it took nine years for an officer to be promoted to captain. Today, officers are often promoted to acting captains with only three years' service and have to bear heavy responsibilities at an early age.

The official responsibilities of an officer in a British regiment in times of peace and before the Independence movement rose and grew, were limited, leaving him possibly more leisure, but at the same time making his training more meticulous and painstaking.

That one-year training with the North Staffordshire Regiment left us very little time—or so it seemed—to us. Mornings were busy with parades and other military duties. The afternoons were taken up in learning Hindustani, which was new to me as I was born in Kolhapur, Maharashtra, and by the time I went to England at the age of ten, my knowledge was limited to Marathi and some smattering of Urdu and Telegu [sic]. But I had been isolated, because of the war, from India, and from close contact with my parents. This isolation in the UK made me forget what little I knew of these languages. The evenings were devoted to games and functions in the Mess, some of them very formal. The usual guests in the Mess were officers of other regiments or important British civilians, but rarely was an Indian civilian invited to the Mess, however important. I, therefore, used to feel very proud on the occasions when my father was invited to a formal function or dinner in the Mess. But I had to provide details to him about the formalities necessary before such invitations were issued, which were quite elaborate. He had formally to call on the Mess, leave two cards—one for commanding officer of the regiment—and thereafter, he received one card in return, and this was followed by an invitation to consider himself an honorary member of the Mess. But it was understood that he would never appear in the Mess unless formally invited to be present. Such was the formality that no important British civilians or other high-ranking persons would be invited to the Mess unless he had formally called, and it was considered 'bad form' for officers of other regiments, or high-ranking civilians or important persons not to call on the Mess soon after their arrival at the station. On a Mess night when guests were present, it was only after the King's Health had been drunk that the severe formalities were relaxed, and everyone was then expected to take part in the 'relaxations', like cockfights or similar strenuous amusements with the officers after the important guests had departed. My father rather enjoyed these evenings because he had a sense of humour and was a jovial man. Of course, no ladies were invited. In the Indian Army, as it exists now, this system has been changed, and ladies are allowed on certain nights an essential relaxation—as the strict exclusion of ladies from the Mess had almost become an anachronism!

Because my home was close—about six miles away—I was permitted one or two evenings a week to visit my parents, but I could not always use my father's car because he was so busy, and often therefore cycled six miles each way, to be able to spend a little time at home.

As my father was a physician to HEH the Nizam, one of the first civilian duties expected of me at Hyderabad was to call on the Nizam. This was quite a ceremony, the time being fixed some days beforehand, and the call, including the presentation of a '*nazar*', dressed formally in a gold embroidered *achkan* (a long buttoned-up coat). The presentation consisted of the offer of gold or silver, according to status, after passing through groups of courtiers and palace officials. The higher ranks of the officials and nobles were required to present '*ashrafis*' (gold coins), while I was let off with five silver rupees. This custom was a relic of the old method of showing loyalty to the local prince, and the nazar was formally to be touched by the prince as a mark of acceptance of the expression of loyalty.

While my father, who was to introduce me, and I waited below a small bare stage flanked by officials, a man in very ordinary clothes appeared on the stage to complete, it appeared to me, some of the arrangements there. To my consternation, the officials all started to bow, and after my father presented his nazar, I realized that it was the Nizam himself, and prepared to do likewise, as soon as my father had introduced me. He talked for some time to my father, and suddenly turned to me and asked, 'You have been abroad a long time, did you get married?'

'No, Your Exalted Highness.' (I remembered fortunately to use the title.)

'Aren't you going to marry a European?'

'No, sir'.

'Why not?'

'Well . . . I am an Indian.'

I heard afterwards that he had been very perturbed by one of his officials returning from a trip abroad with a European wife. I also learnt that the Nizam occasionally appeared in very informal clothes, largely because he was very frugal and abstemious in his habits. Perhaps this was a revulsion from his father, who, it was said, squandered a lot of the wealth of this prosperous state. The then Nizam, however, was a very shrewd and able administrator, fully conversant with all activities in the state.

He was responsible for cement roads in his state probably before any other place in India and even introduced air-conditioned third-class trains on short runs of 100 miles from his capital. It was said that the coaches were kept so clean that the passengers kept their bundles on their laps throughout the journey, for fear of disturbing the set-up.

The revenue and police administrations in his state were also in very capable hands. I believe hardly a single crime, burglary or theft, went untraced in the city of Hyderabad, largely due to the very able criminal investigation abilities of Commissioner of Police Shri Venkatarama Reddy.

The Nizam of course lived, as all Muslim nobility did in those days, with a full complement of wives (in addition to the recognized four) and a very large family.

Purdah was the accepted way of life amongst Muslim families, and my father, when he had to attend to the palace during illnesses, became well-known for his correct diagnoses, despite obtaining information regarding temperatures, pulse rates etc., from invisible patients or through equally invisible friends or attendants.

Purdah was strict amongst Muslim families particularly and influenced the way of life quite appreciably in Hyderabad. Even the sophisticated and educated had to bow to complete segregation in parties and to arranged marriages in their families. Logically, as ladies did not appear before male members even of their own families, marriages often came to be arranged through female intermediaries and attendants, who could gain access to the 'zenana' of a number of families; ultimately, the final arrangements being clinched by exchange of visits of female relatives. The male seemed to deserve no consideration.

My father and mother often took me with them on their social visits in Hyderabad, a place which has always been known for its almost Moghul hospitality. For these visits, we used a carriage until the car replaced it. I was most impressed then by the Falaknuma Palace, where the former prime minister lived, and the hospitality of Salar Jang, a forward-looking man with advanced ideas, who used to entertain us youngsters quite frequently.

The old families of Hyderabad have since been quite adversely affected by the Partition, and some have even split—part going to Pakistan, and part remaining in India. But Hyderabad still carries traces of that gracious living and hospitality for which it was famous at the time of my stay there as a Subaltern.

Postings to units of the Indian Army were made by Army Headquarters. After a year's stay with the British regiment, and I was posted to the Second First (2/1st) Madras Pioneers at Bangalore. Pioneer regiments appeared to be a special feature of the Indian Army, though they were organized like Infantry Battalions and had four rifle companies and Headquarter Company. Each man carried, in addition to his rifle, a spade, pickaxe or a shovel. One of the tasks of the Pioneer Company was to provide communications, make roads etc. for the advance group in the sphere of operations. Consequently, explosive and technical equipment were in the Headquarter Company, formally located on mule transport, and each officer was mounted. Officers in the Pioneer units had, therefore, to undertake an engineering course with a Sapper unit. But they did not receive any senior appointments in the Engineering units, unless they had attained the special knowledge and qualifications required. Selected Pioneer officers sometimes commanded Brigades.

At that time, I was the only Indian officer in the Pioneer Regiment, though within three years others followed. Amongst the newcomers who joined was Sahibzada Amir Ahmad Khan, who, after a few experiments on us, became an excellent cook. During the Second World War, he was a prisoner of war in Germany for some years, and was later in Army Headquarters in Delhi, whence he retired. Another officer was Shri B.K. Kapoor, who later joined the Political Service, held ambassadorial posts abroad and also recently retired. The third was Ghosh, a brilliant officer, who would undoubtedly have reached the highest rank in the army, had he not, unfortunately, been killed in the early days of the war in Singapore.

4

Upper Burma

The regiment soon thereafter moved from Bangalore to Upper Burma. At that time Burma was part of Britain's Indian Empire, which included India, Pakistan, Burma and Ceylon. The Indian Army was liable to serve anywhere within the then Indian Empire, and the Madras Pioneers were posted periodically to Mandalay in Upper Burma, the place glamourized by (Rudyard) Kipling in the words: On the road to Mandalay/ Where the flyin'-fishes play/An' the dawn comes up like thunder outer China 'crost the Bay!

We moved by steamer up the River Irrawaddy, with two large barges attached, one on each side of the steamer. This was a mode of travel which I had not previously experienced, and it was made possible by the fact that the river was very calm at this time of the year. The trip was a most leisurely one, with the steamer moving slowly and halting each day in the evening to pick up a pilot or fuel, or allow the troops to disembark and shop, or for us to undertake a 'flag march', because there had been some problems of non-payment of taxes. In Prome, we called on the deputy commissioner and were entertained by him; while at Yenangyaung, we marched to the oil field. In this leisurely manner, we reached Mandalay about a fortnight later. During the days, which were calm, we were within sight of the banks and saw people working in the rice fields or drawing water from wells. It was mostly the women in their bright coloured lungis who appeared to be working, while the men sat happily by smoking their long pipes. Beyond the green rice fields were the villages and pagodas; whence drifted the voices of children shouting, playing or singing. Young men occasionally climbed long palm trees to collect the local brew, and sometimes another steamer crossed us, and we waved to each other, altogether a serene and peaceful scene.

Mandalay turned out to be a very picturesque place. We were located at Fort Dufferin, which was surrounded by a moat, and were soon inspected by the general officer commanding the Burma District.

These old forts were invariably the strongholds of princes and were usually occupied by the British, as they afforded a suitable place for defence against the local population in case of emergency and also served as a prestigious place to garrison the surrounding areas.

As the army was to undertake garrison duties, we saw little of the local population, and our contact with them was very limited. It was surprising that during the three years we were stationed in Burma, we never met a Burman or Indian of status unless he happened to be a member of the armed forces. Keeping the army away from the local population was part of British policy. Perhaps in this way, they hoped to ensure that the loyalty of Indian troops was not affected. It was also British policy to limit their communications with Junior Commissioned Officers (JCOs) and men to Hindustani, whatever their mother tongue. In my regiment, for example, the mother tongue of the men was Tamil, Telegu, Malayalam or Kannada, but only Hindustani was used in all communications with them. Words of command were in English, but the language of the Indian Army was simple Hindustani. The use of Hindustani not only served as a cementing force for the whole army but also assisted in control, regardless of the part of India to which the men belonged.

It was accepted as an axiom by us that the British kept the army away from the local population as a measure undertaken purely for reasons of prestige, and therefore, this system has not been subsequently followed.

Moreover, we have been toying with the idea of a People's Army. That concept conveys a sense of camaraderie and oneness between the army and the civil, and this is perhaps a satisfying objective. However, the idea of giving military training to all eligible citizens can only be put into force in a totalitarian country. We, a democracy, can only think in terms of utilizing the army for defence and for civilian development work or such other activities that make them closer to the civil population. Unfortunately, though our Defence Budget is high, we have not the funds necessary to maintain a force which can spend a lot of untrained time on development activities. It would be cheaper for us to have trained people to undertake development work and train the army for its regular tasks. We have, I feel, realized that economically it is wasteful to take the newly trained in one task and utilize them for another unless those people are not fully employed in their own tasks. Unfortunately, it has been assumed that military training during peacetime leaves the armed forces with sufficient time on their hands; whereas we have come to learn from the Israeli forces amongst others, how effective an army can be when it is properly trained, and how ineffective an untrained army can become. The Israeli Air Force was so thoroughly trained that, at the first opportunity and in its first assault, it knocked out 60 per cent of the Arab Air Force. The Israelis have learnt that the more highly trained a man is, the more effective he becomes. To put a man trained in military duties to undertake the work of a labour gang or the construction of a dam would prove him to be less effective than the labourer who is used to and trained for the type of work. It would be simpler and more economical to employ a labourer for the work.

To assume that the armed forces have time to devote to other work is to assume that they are so highly trained that they are capable of destroying the enemy as effectively as the Israelis did in their war with the Arabs. But the Pakistan and Chinese wars have proved that we are not so sufficiently trained, and that the more time spent in training the better it will be for our armed forces. Our tanks and aircraft were not as sophisticated as those supplied to the Pakistani forces during the last Indo–Pak conflict. Yet our training in the war of the weapons available to us stood us in good stead.

Had we been better trained, the termination of that war would have been quicker.

In the Chinese war, our forces were not only unaccustomed to that ground but untrained in that terrain; and our training on logistics for that theatre of war left much to be desired.

Socialist countries have realized fully that their armed forces have to spend their time in training for war. In Russia, the common man rarely sees the army except for occasional military or other parades. In China, the People's Army has not accepted too readily the role of supporting the ruling regime in its attempt to retain power; and there have been rumours of a civil strife with the army involved in a not-too-happy state of affairs. The armed forces, therefore, in most countries are left to follow their profession, which keeps them somewhat aloof from local citizens. As far as possible, its task of training is not interfered with even though the army could be used in other civil tasks. The army in India, in addition to its military role, has been used to build houses, assist in the construction of dams and maintain law and order. All these tasks do detract from the main task of training and prevent the soldier from being sufficiently alert to meet the enemy adequately.

In Germany, prior to the war, the army was so trained as to form the nucleus of a force, which was to be very much expanded, and each soldier became so highly specialized that he could be the centre of a cell formed around him of a group of recruits. Every soldier could almost have been an instructor. Prior to the war, the German Army was thus a tight corps of highly trained, very sophisticated troops.

That was why it was so easy to expand when Hitler required the larger forces for his conquests. Furthermore, Germany got together its nucleus of a highly efficient army, while its funds were extremely limited during a period of depression. We, a developing country with limited funds, have to decide whether it is more desirable for us to have a smaller, very highly trained army (like the Israelis), or a larger force with less time spent in training and capable of assisting the civil in its development activities.

We seem to have preferred the latter, largely because the budgets of the civil departments concerned (development or law and order) do not reflect the increasing use of the armed forces for their support. I wonder whether we will continue to prefer the latter despite the experience of the Chinese war. We selected then a general with lots of initiative and plenty of drive, who had been most valuable in assisting the civil administration and had even got troops to construct barracks for themselves at nominal cost and at a very rapid rate—a very enterprising and successful effort. But his combat training had correspondingly been reduced. So, we suffered a mortifying reverse.

We stayed some time in Mandalay, occupied with the usual training tasks during the day and enjoying games during the leisure hours.

Here, we were fortunate enough to have the Burma Military Police, who had also horses on their establishment, and they used them hire us to play polo, at 8 annas a *chukkar*. They also introduced to us a type of local Polo with local rules and local ponies. In riding off, for example, the trick was to get your knee behind your opponent's knee and unseat him—not so dangerous as it sounds, as the ponies were so small that you did not have far to fall.

As part of our training in communications work, we moved further into the jungles of Burma, through Myitkyina, where we split up into three parties. The Headquarters Wing to which I was attached, went to

Sumpra Bum, about 200 miles further north, to construct the Putao Road through dense jungle. This area was in the Triangle, a disturbed area, where trouble could be expected. The Putao Road eventually was to link up with Ledo in Assam, and during the First World War, this road became the escape route, when the Japanese attacked us in Burma. But, during this period, we suffered mainly from bad weather and influenza, which affected all the three units in which we had been divided, and which caused twelve deaths before subsiding. Despite the weather and the epidemic, about thirty miles of road were completed, and experiments were undertaken to ascertain the maximum output for man and for the company.

In the jungles of Burma, our work brought us closer to the troops, and we shared the soldiers' simple but wholesome midday meal of chappatis, dhal [sic] and vegetables. In spite of the fact that we were in the jungle, the evenings in the Mess were formal affairs. The Mess was housed in a large tent where there was a polished table and some chairs. A few silver trophies decorated the table. At night, we wore a Mess kit which consisted of a red monkey jacket (a short jacket down to the waist), a stiff white shirt along with a hard white collar and black bow tie.

We also used blue overalls (long trousers strapped under the boots), wearing with them long black boots with spurs.

Separating the Red Mess jacket and the blue overalls was a scarlet cummerbund. Officers who possessed them wore miniature medals with the appropriate medal ribbons. This formality was observed regularly for six nights a week on the sultriest days in the heart of the jungles of Upper Burma.

On Sundays, the formalities were relaxed. We then wore a civil dinner jacket with a stiff white shirt, hard white collar and black bow tie. Even the bearers attending on us at tables were ceremoniously dressed, white in summer and green in winter, with appropriate cummerbunds and turban bands of our regimental colours.

The proceedings in the Mess were no less formal. We assembled in the anteroom at 8.20 p.m. and the senior officer present in the Mess led us into the dining tent at 8.50 p.m., after the Mess call had been sounded on the bugle. The menu cards were meticulously typed, and the silver was always sparkling. The conversation at the tables was confined to generalities and proceeded with effort. Ladies' names were not mentioned and discussions on politics were disallowed as also were references to regimental matters, which we called 'shop'. Perhaps, all this 'dressing up' was intended to impress the local people. Dress has been a method of impressing people throughout the ages, particularly in times of peace. Gilbert and Sullivan satirized the Colonel of the Dragoons in *Patience* more than a hundred years ago. At that time, the glamour of a uniform was denigrated by long-haired 'aesthetics', as it is being denigrated today in modern Britain by the 'hippies'.

Since Independence, we have continued to keep Mess life fairly formal and have maintained some of the traditions of the corps, but without the outward display—example: punctuality. We have replaced the more resplendent uniforms; but not having many hippies, we are gradually reverting to and recognizing the dignity of 'dress'. Again, we have introduced a less ceremonious atmosphere in the Mess and held five supper nights instead of one a week. Ladies are still rarely allowed in the Mess, but some regiments occasionally have ladies' guest nights to which wives of officers in the regiments are usually invited. The senior subaltern, who is the senior-most lieutenant in the battalion, has an important part to play in upholding its traditions. He carries no official authority, but his commanding officer expects that he will guide newcomers.

Some of us feel that perhaps in the not-too-distant future, Mess dress will be replaced by an even simpler dress jacket with buttoned-up collar. The old Mess uniforms, together with the valuable regimental silver, could be collected and displayed in a museum in such a place as Kharakvasala [sic]. Regimental messes may be abolished and replaced by station clubs. All this would reduce expenditure. In field areas, however, regimental messes would have to continue as a simpler form.

By the time we had completed our stay in Burma, I had served five years with the Madras Pioneers and learnt a great deal about the soldiers with whom I was working and about the soldier in general.

The term 'Madras' was a misnomer because the troops in the Madras Regiment were recruited from all parts of south India except Maharashtra. They were a fine batch of men—hard-working, intelligent and loyal.

The process of learning through which I then passed often caused me some surprise and sometimes discomfiture, but I came to realize that the object of our training was to ensure that we became more effective than the enemy, and our men would follow us in battle even though they may not necessarily espouse the cause for which they were fighting. Our first task, it seemed to me, was to get troops into a habit of obedience almost as a conditioned reflex. If an order was to be obeyed instantly, in the first instance, it had to be such that it would not evoke a negative response, and when once given, it had to be rigidly enforced without deviations. It also took time to appreciate the fact that the men followed the example set by the officers.

Unless an officer's turnout was faultless, he could not easily pull up the *jawans* for being slovenly. Even the best-disciplined troops were apt to break discipline if the examples set were bad. I had occasion to see two platoons on a route march—one very disciplined and the other under a poor officer. The water supply failed to appear at the end of the route march, and the day being a hot one, thirst was acute. Suddenly, the water lorry arrived.

The disciplined platoon continued to stand at ease as they had been ordered to do, but the other platoon broke ranks. This was a very serious breach of discipline. The fact that one platoon had broken ranks and had not been called to order caused the other platoon also to break ranks. One also learnt that the enforcement of discipline was not accomplished by fear. On one occasion, I attempted to ensure that the men returned from leave in time, by issuing threats.

Of course, this had no effect, and nine out of ten men returned late.

The threat of punishment or fear would not—as it became clear—evoke obedience in a soldier. He will be interested in what you are trying to accomplish if he finds that you are genuinely interested in him.

I suppose what we learnt during these years, was how to lead our troops rather than drive them, and it seemed to me, that in the jungles of Upper Burma, we could not have had a better training ground, as we were completely cut off from other activities and remained close to the troops most of the time.

We returned to Bangalore from Burma in December 1928, where we again not only undertook garrison duties but were involved in reorganization to turn us into a Germs of Pioneers from the 1 April 1929. Here, I also passed the examination, which qualified me to be promoted to captain, and a technical engineering course, for which the letter 'Q' was added to my name in the army list, indicating that I had qualified in engineering duties.

Early in 1930, we had the opportunity to undertake further work in connection with the Thippagondanahalli water supply project in Bangalore, which virtually turned Bangalore from a water-deficit area to a surplus one. In this project, we covered the distance in one march, the officers marching with the men, travelling twenty-five miles in a day. We had also to take serious precautions against a cholera epidemic. The neighbourhood of our place of work being of very hilly nature, we also had an excellent opportunity of practising mountain warfare.

A number of officers had, in the meantime, joined us. Anis Ahmad Khan, Baljit Singh and Walawalker had already been with us in Burma, but we were joined in Bangalore by S.K. Ghosh, a brilliant officer who had been attached to the Second Yorkshire Regiment and was posted to Corps Headquarters and Captain Rana Joda Jung Bahadur. He had joined as a lieutenant in 1913, had already distinguished himself in the First World War in France, being awarded the MC and MBE, had been attached to the Gorkha Rifles and the Sikh Pioneers, had been appointed as a commandant to the Tehri Garhwal State Sappers and served as an honorary ADC to HE the Viceroy. Most of us young officers were then bachelors, but Captain Rana, having a family, added a great deal to the social life of the battalion.

5

First Steps Towards Indianization

Pioneer regiments had a long history, and in fact, gave birth to some Sapper and Miner units. The 2/1st Madras Pioneers had been raised as early as 1758, and when I joined the army on the 30 August 1923, there were nineteen Pioneer regiments in existence.

The term 'Pioneer' has been defined in the dictionary as 'one that goes before to clear the way', and Pioneer regiments were in fact infantry who carried the necessary tools and received suitable training to enable them to open up communications in advance in hostile territory. They were normally able to look after themselves in hostile country while engaged in communication tasks.

(Lt Col W.B.P.) Tugwell, in his history, points out that service in the Pioneers was much sought after by officers joining the Indian Army because of their reputation, the frequency with which they saw active service and the variety of their work. This fact has been well supported by Field Marshal Sir Claud Jacob. In fact, one Infantry Regiment was converted to Pioneers as a mark of appreciation for their gallantry in war at Zariba. Pioneers were used to supplement Engineering Field Companies, and with assistance, they could be employed for road marking, plate laying or laying of light railways. In addition to taking part in the fighting in the areas where they were located, Pioneers did excellent work in Africa and Asia, in building defences on the banks of the Tigris, laying a pipeline from the Izzakhai Canal, draining a mosquito-ridden marsh at Bahret and Wadi Ishkar, in laying a light railway to Suakin, in distinguishing themselves in the fighting at Tofrek on one of the few occasions when a British Square was broken, and in building up various defences and communications mostly under fire on the North-West Frontier. Pioneers therefore, had a very chequered and colourful history. One battalion, a Marino Battalion, had started off its career in the Bombay Marines, working on gallivants and vessels in the service of the East India Company in the harbour of Bombay and taking part in the fighting involved on the coast and as far away as Burma.

It even got involved in the only engagement between the Indian Marines and an American National Ship *Peacock*, just after the Anglo–American war had concluded, and peace had been signed. This battalion which eventually became the 121st Pioneers gave its name to 'Marine Lines' in Bombay. Needless to say, many of the officers and men of the Pioneers received decorations for bravery, such as the VC or MC, or for distinguished service, such as the DSO or IDSM.

During the First World War and after, the role of the Pioneers were especially important because it enabled the troops while fighting to open communications and bring up artillery and other noble equipment, sufficiently forward to make it effective against a concentration of enemy troops. But naturally, as aircraft began to take the role of long-range guns and warfare became more mobile, particularly with the use of tracked vehicles, the role of the Pioneers began to dwindle. In the early days when regular troops were not stationed permanently in tribal territory for carrying out punitive or other operations, there was a great deal of work for Pioneer units in opening up troublesome areas.

Under the system of permanent positioning, the condition altered completely as the local situation was more settled. Communications were then more permanently established with civilian labour or by special communication units. Subsequently, the work of communications became more and more technical and had to be relegated to the Engineering units which could execute or supervise technical work much more satisfactorily, particularly as the Pioneers were not so qualified for carrying out highly technical tasks as the Engineers.

The end of these multipurpose units, which have had such a varied and colourful history, became inevitable and all Pioneer units had to be disbanded. On 21 October 1932, my regiment, which had a tradition of well over a century and half, was disbanded, and the men were drafted to the Madras Sappers or given special pensions. On 10 February 1933, all Pioneers of the Indian Army ceased to exist.

The King's Commissioned Indian Officers (KCIOs) belonging to the Madras Pioneers were offered the option of joining the Madras Sapper units or going to infantry units. Because of the greater mobility of the army and larger mechanization with tracked and smaller vehicles, the Sapper units were naturally to follow the advance troops and would not see so much of the fighting. Moreover, the Madras Sappers were stationed at Bangalore, a very pleasant town, a family station, where life would be very comfortable. In many ways, this was an inducement for us to select the Madras Sapper unit. However, I felt that unless one received training in combat, one would not have full training in the total role of the army, particularly the most important role. Feeling, I presume, that it would be more adventurous to be in an infantry unit, particularly, if it was posted in the frontier or other combat areas, I opted for the infantry, and I was posted to the 4/19 Hyderabad Regiment at Fort Sandeman on the North-West Frontier. During this period, I experienced no difficulty in transition, from the point of view of professional duties to the infantry; my knowledge of tactics and weapons was up to standard, and I was able to adapt myself easily to all infantry duties.

The 4/19th Hyderabad Regiment was one of the eight India-sized units, and at the time of my joining the battalion there were several KCIOs in it. These included, amongst others, Captain Naranjan Singh Gill, Thimayya, Azam Khan, Bahadur Singh and Yadunath Singh.

After the fall of Singapore, Captain Naranjan Singh Gill became a prisoner of war in Japanese hands and became one of the leaders of the Indian National Army (INA). Despite that, he suffered a great deal because of the Japanese. Thimayya became Chief of the Army Staff. Bahadur Singh after completion of his tenure as Army Commander, Central Command, was appointed lieutenant governor of Himachal Pradesh. (Bahadur Singh had also been a prisoner of war in Japanese hands but was not connected with the INA movement.) Azam Khan went to Pakistan. Yadunath Singh became a Divisional Commander in Jammu and Kashmir. After retiring, he joined the police.

The 4/19th Hyderabad Regiment was a fine unit, and British officers were very helpful to us. The regiment comprised Kumaonis, Jats and Ahirs. The commanding officers of these regiments were men of high calibre and guided and educated us well in our profession. One of our commanding officers was Lt Col Wilfred Lloyd—an exceptionally fine soldier, dedicated to his work. He drove his officers hard, particularly, it seemed to me, is adjutant—a course which I did not relish very much at the time. I later realized how much I had benefited from working under him.

There were at that time two classes of Indian officers in Indian regiments, the KCIOs and the Viceroy's Commissioned Officers (VCOs). The KCIOs were commissioned as second lieutenants, while VCOs were commissioned as jamadars, now known as nayak subedars, which was not a Class I gazetted rank. VCOs were usually soldiers promoted from the ranks or selected from persons with a little lower educational qualification. They commanded platoons of some thirty men and were selected especially for leadership qualities and given special training in the regiments. They were privileged to be saluted by the jawans but were not entitled to use the officers' Mess. KCIOs, on the other hand, commanded companies of four platoons, were selected from people of higher educational qualifications, or with important family backgrounds, and were trained in the regiment after a course at Sandhurst.

The British officers kept in close touch with the VCOs, who formed their principal liaison with the men. Often, the senior-most VCO, known as the subedar major, was the personal confidant of the commanding officer and kept him informed of all happenings in the regiment. These VCOs formed the backbone of the junior officers of the regiment and have been called since Independence, JCOs.

While the VCOs formed the group on which British officers relied, KCIOs became a somewhat disturbing group. They replaced, in fact, the British officers and the men seemed to turn more to them in their regimental work and in their other activities. This caused a subtle, if not marked change in the regimental set-up. It seemed to have caused the Army Headquarters some concern, particularly as, with seniority, the KCIOs posted to a regiment might eventually take over almost complete control of that unit. Army Headquarters, therefore, thought it advisable to limit this form of Indianization and devised a plan whereby only eight out of fifty regiments would thus have KCIOs posted to them. These regiments consisted of two cavalry regiments, four infantry battalions and one regiment of Pioneers.

By this ingenious plan, Indian officers would be confined to a few regiments and their influence in the army as a whole would be restricted.

It was calculated that provided Indianization worked according to plan. It would be 1952 before these eight regiments would be completely Indianized. By that time, the army might have grown a little, and these eight regiments would form a small proportion only of the total Indian Army. At this rate of Indianization, it would take many much years to Indianize the existing Army.

In 1927, the Skeen Committee, which included some eminent patriotic public men, like Pandit Motilal Nehru and the founder of Pakistan.

Mr M.A. Jinnah recommended abandoning the eight unit scheme and replacing it with one, which provided for half the total cadre of officers in the army to be composed of Indians by 1952.

The Indianization of the army's remaining half was not even mentioned.

By then, I had completed ten years of service and was beginning to feel somewhat frustrated. Financially, I was in no better position than I was when I first joined the army, and my prospects appeared to be not too rosy, as the best I could hope for was to retire as a Lt Col. Again, my father had been ill, and I had had little opportunity to be with him. I thought several times of giving up my career in the army. Some of my colleagues and friends advised me to apply for the political service, which might lead to greater opportunities and a more settled life. However, at that time, a wave of nationalism began to grip the nation, and Gandhiji and Panditji had aroused the imagination of the masses. However loyal one was to one's profession, the thought of self-rule and self-government caught the imagination. I remembered the advice that my uncle, Shamrao Kelavkar, had offered to me, saying that India would need people trained in every aspect of life. Perhaps this influenced me to continue in the army and the profession in which I was being trained. Even according to the Skeen Committee's recommendations, however, by 1952, when I would be climbing to the top of the ladder of the profession, only half the army would be composed of KCIOs, and presumably very few Indians would be in Army Headquarters or in posts of importance.

In actual fact, India took over the whole of its army and officered it completely five years earlier than 1952. It was a remarkable achievement shattering all the carefully worked-out steps towards achieving partial Indianization at a much later date. The achievement was remarkable because Indians had never worked in some of the higher posts in the Army Headquarters and not even in some of the top posts in the commands. Not only, therefore, were they unfamiliar with the work involved in these posts, but they had not the slightest training. One of the main causes for the effectiveness of the army in India which we learnt through the British conquest of India, was the tough way in which a soldier trained for the job he was to undertake so that at the time of need, he would be able to meet its requirements. Training, therefore, has been almost a sine qua non of every activity in the army. The takeover in 1947 had not only been sudden but had been accelerated towards the end, and the plans for the takeover themselves were not complete. It certainly placed a heavy responsibility on junior officers, particularly those who had to assume commands of regiments, and who averaged only seven to nine years of service. That the army has answered all calls made on it since Independence and has been at all times loyal to the country, speaks volumes for the calibre and integrity of the officers and men who composed it.

6

The Administration

Having made up my mind to continue in the army, I attended several army courses of instruction and passed the examination for promotion to major. It was now decided, largely because of the recommendations of the Skeen Committee, that by 1933, India should have her own Military College at Dehradun on the same lines as Sandhurst. This meant that the intake of Indian cadets into the army would be greater.

An unhappy result of this scheme was that although the Military College at Dehradun was staffed by selected British officers and sergeants, and although the standard of instruction was to be on the level of Sandhurst. Indian cadets, on being commissioned, were treated as a different class. They not only received lower pay, though they were Class I gazetted officers, but they were called Indian Commissioned Officers (ICOs) instead of KCIOs. Furthermore, the difference was aggravated when ICOs began to be absorbed in units as platoon commanders in place of VCOs, while KCIOs were taken as commanders or second-in-command of companies. A gulf was thus created between KCIOs and ICOs, and this naturally created resentment against the former KCIOs.

To my mind, this gap was completely artificial because the cadets who were chosen as ICOs were selected based on a very stiff competition, and they seemed to be of as high a calibre as those who had been selected to be trained at Sandhurst as KCIOs. I presume that the difference was intended to indicate the difference in training between Sandhurst and Dehradun, but I am inclined to doubt whether this difference was serious enough to warrant the creation of a different category of officers, or whether any difference in training could not have been overcome. The disadvantage of being trained in Sandhurst was that the cadet lost some time in absorbing Western culture and customs—a process we had to pass through if we had not already been living in or trained in England.

This process naturally absorbed a good deal of time, which could have been spent on military training.

Those who had already been in England or received training in the OTC or Other Paramilitary Organizations, had also become accustomed to the type of training given in Sandhurst, particularly on parades. As an example, because of the influence of the First World War, there was no hesitation in 'ticking off' persons who had made mistakes, and these tickings off were often very crude. We, Indians, as a rule, not often accustomed to such methods of instruction, resented these tickings off.

This can be seen even with 'labour' today. Workmen would prefer to be told the correct way to do things than to be told that their task had been performed incorrectly. So, instruction at Dehradun was absorbed, in my opinion, a little more quickly than instruction at Sandhurst. Moreover, there appeared to be no reason why Dehradun, being officered and staffed by British officers and sergeants, could not have been made equal to Sandhurst. The Kingston Military School in Canada, located in Kingston, was started along the same lines, as Sandhurst; but thereafter it obtained the reputation of being one of the best military schools in the world. There was no reason why Dehradun could not follow suit.

Again, I am not at all sure that the product of Dehradun was in any manner inferior to the product of Sandhurst. There have been many outstanding products of Dehradun, the average level being, in my opinion, in no way inferior to those trained at Sandhurst. Of course, in later years, the recruitment was of a much larger number of officers and the selection was thus not limited to the very few.

It is unfortunate that we failed to tackle this problem effectively, even after Independence. We senior KCIOs would have helped to remove this bitterness, had we been successful in persuading the government to agree that such an anomaly must be removed. Why then did we allow matters to drift? Perhaps we did not think too deeply about this problem, as we were too junior then to oppose policy decisions at a political level, or it may be that political expediency outweighed administrative considerations.

Presumably, because this artificial gulf had been accepted by the political pundits of the day, a similar differentiation was made on the government side. Before Independence, officers of the Indian Civil Service were recruited and trained in England; and after Independence, officers of the Indian Administrative Services were recruited and trained in India. There was a marked difference in their privileges and emoluments. Looking back, it would appear that the British policy of reducing certain privileges in the service terms of Indians in the army had tended to establish rival social groups amongst Indians in the service. It was regrettable that such a policy was introduced also in the civil services. After Independence, possibly considerations of social equality dictated the continuance of the reduced pay for ICOs in the armed forces.

Anyway, this created an artificial division in the ranks of service officers, which certainly the army could not afford, for homogeneity and discipline are essential concomitants of a good fighting force.

I hope now that when all the KCIOs have retired from the army, the army will be a more uniform group.

But the intervening years have been crucial. Thanks to the character and sense of duty shown by KCIOs and ICOs, the functioning of the ground forces after Independence has not suffered as it might otherwise have done.

On 30 January 1933, I received the tragic news of my father's death. This placed a heavy responsibility on my mother's shoulders; for, apart from J.M. and I, who were away from home on government service, the rest of the children were very young. However, my mother accepted the loss bravely. She closed down our house in Hyderabad and moved temporarily to Punjab, to stay with J.M. who had entered the ICS in the year 1928 and was then at Rupar (Punjab).

There has always been a certain amount of rivalry between the armed forces and the civil services. I believe that a change of conditions or procedures can lessen or increase such tensions. For example, the ICS have quite inadvertently come in for a lot of envy on account of their better conditions of service. In our struggling democracy, cooperative effort and combined drive from the services are prime conditions for rapid progress. But it is unfortunate that after Independence, tensions between the civil and military have tended to increase. Perhaps some of these tensions were aggravated by the inevitable change in the position of the Commander-in-Chief, who prior to Independence was, next to the viceroy, the most important member of the

Executive Council. Thereafter, the farmhand of the armed forces has rightly been vested in the President of India, who is the supreme commander. The Defence Secretariat, which previously had worked under the Commander-in-Chief, is now under the defence minister.

The time-honoured principle of civil control of defence matters is sound. But it is in the exercise of this control that tensions between the services appear to have increased. What is civil control? Surely not controlled by civil servants, whose task is to provide a secretariat to the defence minister. It means, necessarily, political control, which is fundamental to our democracy. Such political control must be that of the minister, without the Defence Secretariat working as a sort of controller general of the three Service Headquarters. During the early years of Independence, defence policy was a new subject to most politicians, and only such civilians as Chandulal Trivedi, H.M. Patel, H.C. Sarin had the experience of its formulation. These officers were of considerable value in the early years, until the proper role of the defence minister was fully assumed. They made a number of decisions and quick ones, of which any defence organization could be proud. But subsequent secretaries appear to have relegated control and coordinating measures to the secretariat itself. The function of the Defence Secretariat has now to be redefined, and a system evolved, as in the UK or the US, for the services to work under a unified structure, under one apex.

Those who work in the Government of India secretariat are to be admired. They have not only to be administrators, but administrators with special aptitudes, largely because of the outmoded organization of the secretariat, and the changing phases of the administrative and political scene.

The organization of the secretariat was based on the system adopted when ministries were few, members limited and administration geared to a static form of government. Noting on files could be used to express divergent opinions, display one's ability in the twists of the English language, or even emphasize the importance of the writer or his views. When coordination was required, it was undertaken by passing the file up and down each ministry, and sometimes across to another ministry (where it made its inevitable journey up and down), and this leisurely process was tolerably acceptable, as time was not necessarily a factor of importance. However, it required a great deal of skill to get work accomplished in time when the tempo changed into that of a developmental government's, burdened with a somewhat inflexible, antiquated and bureaucratic form of administration. The skilled secretariat officer had to devise where the power of decision in another ministry really lay—in the minister, the deputy minister, the secretary or his deputies. He then had to devise an informal system where he could be assured of coordination and acceptance by the other ministries involved. This was no easy task when the sphere of influence of each ministry was not too clearly demarcated. He had to obtain the inevitable financial approval. He had also to overcome the obstructionism arising from the corruption of power and the tyranny of the petty official. Getting a project through was, therefore, no easy task.

Various ministers had their way of attempting to get things done; some by caustic measures and others by sweeping out existing administrators and replacing them. A few, like Pandit Jawaharlal Nehru, had the knack of getting quickly to grips with problems that came up before him. I would not have given up the chance of working for him for anything else on earth. He was a wonderful character, a genius with intimate knowledge of men and affairs and a warm heart. It was also a pleasure working for Lal Bahadur Shastri, who achieved results by quiet, patient listening and by coordination and consensus.

Unfortunately, a few of the administrators who were especially adept at secretarial 'skills' did not find favour with their political 'bosses'; and some fell under the tyranny of the anachronistic post-mortems of the Public Accounts

Committee of Parliament's decision-making. They, therefore, tended to be shunned, making the secretariat system more and more 'bureaucratic' in the worst sense. Its officers deserve praise for how they carried on the administration despite such adverse conditions and in the face of substantial opposition. In the toils of the system, India has given up a number of able administrators ([A.D.] Gorwala, H.M. Patel, [Subrahmanya] Bhoothalingam, to name a few), whom it could ill afford to lose.

It now requires not a team of brilliant individualists, but competent, quiet workers, who are coordinators as well as administrators, to fill the gaps.

7

March towards Independence in a World-Torn Era

On the 29 July 1934, I married Rajkumari, the eldest daughter of Major J.R. Kochhar of the Indian Medical Service (IMS), who hailed from the Punjab and was stationed at that time at the Military Hospital, Meerut.

I had had a glimpse of her one year earlier in Lahore but had never spoken to her. My wife's mother tongue was Punjabi, and as I had no knowledge of that language, I spoke to her for the first time on our wedding day in English. Some years later, my wife told me that had she known that I did not know Punjabi, she might never have agreed to marry me, for the family belonged to Gujerat [sic], in the Punjab, and everyone she knew spoke Punjabi. I am still unable to converse in Punjabi, so we have compromised on Hindi and English.

The regiment moved shortly thereafter from Fort Sandeman (a non-family station) to Quetta, where my wife was to join me. However, at 3 a.m. on 31 May 1935, I was an 'umpire' on a night exercise with a Sikh battalion outside Quetta. At one moment we were marching along a road, and in the next one, all of us were struggling as a confused mass on the ground. This had seemed strange and even amusing at the same time.

At the end of the exercise, we marched back to the cantonment. The first house we saw en route elicited some amused comments, as it appeared to be squatting flat on the ground. The amusement turned first to incomprehension, as other houses appeared in the distance in a similar posture with a lot of rubble nearby, and then our feelings turned to concern and anguish as every house appeared to have collapsed and some buildings were on fire. It then dawned on us that the incident at 3 a.m. had been a severe earthquake and a major disaster. As we approached the city, we saw that almost the whole of it had collapsed and that fire was raging in many parts, and men, women and children were shrieking under the debris.

We quickened our pace and reached our barracks; but the destruction had been so great and the shock so complete . . . without warning that confusion had reigned supreme, till the early hours of the afternoon.

The general officer, Commander-in-Chief, Western Command, was on leave in England, and Gen. Karslake was then officiating, who controlled the situation very quickly despite a lack of communications, organized relief measures and got into direct communication by telephone with Whitehall from the lawns of the Quetta Club, whence he directed operations. It was only towards the evening that the extent of the disaster became fully known, and the relief operations commenced.

The army commander, being on leave, sent his sympathies on hearing of the earthquake and did what little he could by making his residence available for any emergency. Of course, his house was also in ruins.

Gen. Karslake was knighted for quickly and ably organizing relief. Our battalion received the highest praise for outstanding humanitarian work, and the men reacted with spontaneous energy, working very long hours, without thought of their own comfort or wants.

The destruction and misery elicited human sympathy from all parts of India. Yet, of the people who were affected, some behaved very callously. We had, for example, to forcibly prevent a man trying to remove a gold ring from a dying woman's finger; and another from searching a safe for hidden wealth, regardless of the feelings of those half buried underneath. The army, which had been immediately deployed on rescue work, had to divert its attention from time to time to prevent looting.

Fate works in mysterious and peculiar ways. Several of my friends became homeless overnight. A well-respected elder from my wife's family was to have left Quetta the night before, having come there on a visit but was persuaded by his friends to remain a night longer, for that fated night. He was buried in the debris. One of the survivors was a very young child—hardly able to speak—who found wandering in the city alone. The nurses of the hospital had considerable difficulty in persuading her to put on her clothes after a bath until they realized that she had been accustomed to being powdered before being clothed! No trace of her family was found.

Rehabilitation work was very strenuous as it entailed not only removing the debris and rescuing those who might have still remained alive but also burying and cremating the dead, caring for the wounded, clearing the area to prevent an epidemic and ensuring proper sanitation—drainage and communications—almost setting up a new city. The influx of people from outside had to be screened, because of lack of accommodation, even though every bit of help was of material value. Fortunately, the earthquake did not affect the cantonment so seriously. The army designed temporary structures and quickly set up tented accommodations. Later, the temporary structures, which consisted of brick walls and brick chimneys with tented roofs, proved very valuable in keeping out some of the intense cold winds of the Quetta winter; and the 'Wana Huts', the name given for those improvised tented accommodation, proved of great value and were greatly in demand. Recently, I heard a civil officer's comment on these Wana Huts, which implied that the army was required to live under canvas for a period as part of their training and therefore had adopted these huts to be able to say that they were under canvas. The fact is that army accommodation, particularly family accommodation, was normally non-existent, and these huts were improvised shelters made to meet the cold of Quetta winter and to accommodate family there. In fact, I considered myself lucky to be allotted one of these Wana Huts. I invited the civilian, who made the comment on the Wana Huts, to spend the winter under canvas in Quetta, which, I was amused to hear, he found himself unable to accept.

In the meantime, our first child, a girl, Pimmy, had been born at Meerut, but Quetta had now become a non-family station for the time being because of the shortage of accommodation. However, early in April 1937, my regiment moved to Secunderabad, where my second child, Satish, was born.

To celebrate his arrival, I invited the young officers of my regiment to my house. Whilst standing around the cot, one of the officers, Khushwaqt-ul-Mulk, looking at the baby, said, 'You poor little ICO', inferring that Satish could never become a KCIO like his father, and emphasizing the distinction between the KCIO and the ICO. Satish later joined the army as an ICO.

War clouds were now gathering in the west; and we Indian officers expected that some of us would be involved on the lines of the 1914–18 war, particularly if the war became prolonged. It is only during war that the soldier can bring his training into practice and can even update it. Few of us look for war, but we realize that for people under colonial administration, war alone can bring us closer to modern weapons and up-to-date strategy and tactics. Many soldiers and civilians had written theories on tank warfare, the use of air etc., and Germany had by then evolved the 'Blitzkrieg' to overwhelm the Czechoslovaks. Though we had read Liddell Hart and others, such reading does not bring us the direct experience that war would. At the same time, war would bring death, misery and destruction. To say the least, our feelings were mixed.

As war became more imminent, my regiment was moved from Secunderabad.

But we were sent to Singapore, embarking from Madras on the SS *Telwa* on 2 August 1939. As we were the first troops to move out of India, we attracted a lot of attention and publicity. But it seemed to me that we were moving in the wrong direction. War clouds were gathering in the west, and Singapore appeared to be many miles distant from any likely theatre of activity. But we were to form a part of force Emergency Military Unit (EMU), presumably to replace British garrisons in Singapore, which in their turn were moving west, in anticipation of possible outbreak of hostilities there. My wife's father, Lt Col J.R. Kochhar (IMS), and her eldest brother, Capt. Kumar Kochhar

(Madras Sappers), also received orders to join the EMU in Singapore.

Apart from the multifarious duties of adjutant to the battalion, which kept me very fully occupied, I was faced with the problem of finding accommodation for the family . . . a problem faced now by most of our officers, particularly those deployed on our very lengthy borders. My wife was lucky enough to be able to move with our two small children to her father's house in Lahore.

The anxiety which our young women have to suffer in such circumstances is difficult to visualize. Latterly, our officers and men of the army have also had occasion to move out of cantonments several times, at short notice, leaving their families behind. The radio and newspapers have been the families' only quick means of receiving information about their husbands or sons, and families have waited patiently for a letter or a telegram. Regiments, which have recently moved out, have been deployed on the border and have had to stay out for long periods, under battle conditions. Possibly a tent, a bush or a tree has been their only shelter from the blazing sun or torrential rains. As life on the border is dull and monotonous, commanders have also had to use skill and ingenuity to maintain the morale of their officers and men. After Independence, our relations with our neighbours have, if anything, worsened, and troops are being stationed almost permanently on the border without accommodation. And even when they have returned to their peace stations, family accommodation has not been available. This is an unsatisfactory state of affairs and is very detrimental to morale. I believe that lack of accommodation is the greatest single factor against officer recruitment and steps must be taken to build more and more accommodations to house the families of our officers and men, especially of those looking after our new, long and vulnerable borders. I am happy to say that the government is fully alive to the problem, and more and more accommodation is being built in cantonments all over India.

Again, frequent transfers to non-family stations and sometimes even to family stations, bring in their wake several problems for married officers, especially those with school-going children. Sometimes such transfers take place in the middle of the academic year. This is disturbing, as a choice has to be made, either for the children to change schools mid-term (which also involves changing books) or for the family to be separated. It often happens that the wife has to be left behind to fend for herself and find her own accommodation, entailing expenditure on two separate establishments and posing additional economic problems.

If our army is deployed too frequently on the border, without coming to grips with the enemy, it will lose its fighting qualities and its highly developed tactical effectiveness. Perhaps it may be possible to organize a paramilitary force, similar to the Assam Rifles, working directly under army control, (but not under dual control as now), to man the border at short notice. Such forces should be trained for a fast-moving, hard-hitting mobile role, and their standard of leadership at all levels must be of a high order so that they can operate effectively and independently across mountains, countering, if necessary, enemy infiltrations in their rear. They should also have the ability and equipment to ensure that vital information is obtained quickly.

I had been in Singapore with my regiment for hardly five months when I received orders to report to the Indian Military Academy (IMA), Dehradun, as an instructor. I was the first Indian officer to be given this honour. I was happy to return to India, as at that time we saw no indication in Singapore that the Japanese had any intention of waging war against us. Little did we know then, how future events would shape. In December 1939, I returned to India.

On reporting at the IMA, I was attached for a month to an Indian regiment in Razmak on the North-West Frontier, to learn the special technique required for conducting operations on the frontier. I accompanied this battalion on various missions in Razmak and gathered experience of active soldiering in tribal territory. I carried out similar

missions later when I commanded my own battalion at
Mir Ali and Razmak in 1943 and 1944. Our work on the
frontier taught us to make good use of ground under enemy
fire, both by day and night, and to move along the best
route. We also learnt, in a practical way, the principle of fire
and movement. These were useful lessons for conducting
operations later in the jungles of Burma. Work at the
IMA was essentially training cadets, closely resembling
Sandhurst in syllabus and methods. The experience gained
in working under battle conditions and the practical
knowledge of soldiering on the frontier, proved to be of
utmost value in launching me in my duties as an 'instructor'.
The subject allotted to me was 'frontier warfare'. Batches
of cadets were taken out to camp at Sahiya, near Chakrata,
where a school for teaching mountain warfare, had been
established. I was also placed in charge of the academy's
hockey team. My wife was keen on tennis; so sometimes
we made up a four with other instructors and their wives,
or with cadets.

I was promoted while at the academy, from company
officer to company commander, and then a group
commander. A group commander was in charge of two
companies of some 150 cadets each. Later, a special
Military Wing was introduced at the academy for the
British Army. This enabled some of the pressure to be taken

off Sandhurst, by transferring the training of some British officers, destined for the Indian Army, to Dehradun. It also bore out my contention that there was no real distinction between the KCIO and the ICO, as the training at Dehradun was now apparently accepted as equivalent to Sandhurst. I subsequently had many opportunities to visit Dehradun since; and find that the courses of instruction and training continue to be of the highest standard. I believe that the products of the Indian Military Academy, Dehradun, are as good as almost any Military Academy in the world.

On 7 December 1941, Japan came into the war against the United States. This naturally brought in Britain on the side of US, and India, as part of the British Empire, also became involved in the war with Japan. For her defence against Japan, India depended on Singapore as her bastion in the east.

By the surprise attack on Pearl Harbour and the capture of the Philippines by the Japanese, Singapore was considerably weakened. Singapore's defences faced the sea, with the land approaches in the rear, undefended. Further, the Japanese had organized an elaborate espionage system in Singapore with the help of the local Chinese inhabitants living in the city, who gave up-to-date and accurate information on the day-to-day movements of British and Indian troops. Again, no one then believed that an attack could be mounted on Singapore by land, because of the extraordinarily long lines of communication through an inhospitable country. So, Singapore was unprepared from a land attack by Japanese—the bastion found itself unprepared, and it fell unexpectedly and rapidly.

After the fall of Singapore, the Japanese drive towards Rangoon gained momentum. Rangoon was evacuated on 7 March 1942, and thousands of Indians began their track to India through the difficult jungles of the Arakan. Here, the forethought of the British in building communications became apparent. The fall of Rangoon had brought the war close to us, as Gen. Alexander's forces withdrew to the Eastern Gates of India, after fighting retreating battles in Burma against overwhelming odds, over such routes which we had helped to build.

Defence measures had, therefore, to be concentrated in India, but full support for the war was lacking because Britain had failed to exercise sufficient effort in getting India to commit herself in the early days. This was unfortunate, as in September 1939, a wave of sympathy for England and against the totalitarian countries and against Hitler, had spread throughout the country, and there was a general feeling that India could have been easily persuaded to declare war against totalitarian aggression. But technically, India was at war when Britain was, and India was deemed committed without her leaders being consulted. It had even provided the troops which had helped delay the first German attack on Paris. The principal political party, the Indian National Congress, which was then fighting for India's political freedom, felt that as Britain was not prepared to recognize India's freedom after the war, Indians would come more and more to believe that this was not India's war despite Japan entering it, and the war reaching the very borders of the country.

It was against this background that, in 1942, Gandhiji launched the Quit India Movement, which later that year turned to overt action. So, the relations between the British and the Congress became further strained.

In retrospect, events appear to have been the natural outcome of the failure to get the cooperation of the Congress leaders, when it was still possible, in the early days of the war.

In spite of these political differences inside the country, events in India moved fast. With Hitler's invasion of Poland, the army in India was mobilized in September 1939, and Indian troops began arriving in Suez from October 1939 onwards. The role assigned to this force was the Middle East and Africa, but some ancillary units were sent to France to provide transport cover to the British Expeditionary Forces. Among them was Capt.

Anis Ahmed Khan, who was earlier with us in the Madras Pioneers. During the retreat from Dunkirk, he was taken prisoner and remained in Germany throughout the war. I was disappointed that although we were the first troops to leave India for overseas duty, we did not contact the enemy till 1941, whereas those who left India after us, contacted the enemy almost immediately.

During the Second World War, Indian Army units fought gallantly in France, Italy, Africa, Middle East, Malaya, Burma and Indonesia, whilst at the same time protecting the North-West Frontier of India and carrying out their role of internal security within the country. These duties necessitated tremendous expansion. In October 1939, the strength of the army was approximately half a million, whilst in October 1944, it rose to over 2 million. Throughout this momentous period, our troops made substantial contributions to the Allied cause in the different theatres of war.

About this time, news reached India of the formation of the Indian National Army (INA), under the dynamic leadership of Subhas Chandra Bose.

When Singapore fell on 15 February 1942, some 60,000 Indian troops had joined what was named the 'Indian National Army'. This was to be the army of free India, with a provisional government under the presidency of Subhas Chandra Bose. But according to British Military

Law, these men had committed the offences of mutiny, desertion and waging war against the king. For them, therefore, it was a very serious step particularly as their comrades, that is men of sister battalions of the same regiment and drawn from the same stock, were winning glory and admiration for their fellow soldiers, British and American in North Africa, France and Italy.

Perhaps, the reason why some of these troops went over to the enemy was because of nationalistic fervour. Were these men right? These soldiers were recruited in the INA under the command of Capt. Mohan Singh, who made his choice from a genuine conviction and was prepared to suffer, and did, in fact, suffer for his beliefs. Further, the personality of Subhas Chandra Bose was overwhelming. But, in Military Law, the offence of mutiny cannot be condoned. This fact is of interest to the future leaders of our army. To new India, the Indian Army can only be a valuable asset if it preserves its loyalty and discipline. This question is of particular interest because there have been talks of independent states. It will equally be an offence if a soldier, in the event of a conflict with a state, prefers to fight for the state to which he belongs rather than to India as a whole.

In December 1942, my name appeared in Indian Army Orders, to attend the Staff Course at the Command and Staff College, Quetta. About the same time my posting orders came through appointing me to command an infantry battalion. I preferred this posting to an appointment of the staff. 'Staff' led to closer contact with senior commanders and gave an insight into higher military thinking. On the other hand, 'command' meant association with troops on active device, an experience to which I had been looking forward. I had had ample experience of regimental work; and was now anxious to 'command', particularly under conditions of modern war. So, I opted for 'command' in the hope of proceeding with a unit to a theatre of war.

The 'command' came on 27 December 1942, of a newly raised battalion, the 6/19 Kumaon Regiment, which was then located at Bannu, on the North-West Frontier of India. The brigade commander felt that the battalion was not in very good shape, and I was given the task of preparing it for war in the shortest possible time. The regiment had good officers, six British and five Indian, the VCOs were men of experience; and the soldiers were young and active.

What was required, however, was coordinated work and hard and intensive training; stress was also to be placed on discipline and firepower, as we had then to learn the special techniques required for conducting operations on the frontier, appreciating that the Pathans had a reputation for springing surprises, that they were good marksmen and very mobile on steep slopes. The Pathans carried merely a rifle and a bit of food. They were tough, used to the terrain and consequently very active. We, on the other hand, were handicapped with heavy boots and equipment and were not so mobile. We thus gave the enemy the advantage of mobility, and freedom to select the point of attack. The Pathans were also very clever with their ambushes, to which the only answer was to keep fully alert. An example of alertness is given in advance through Shakti Tangi at a time when no enemy had been seen. The intelligence officer of the South Wales Border Regiment spotted a cleft in the very close horizon, through which he could see daylight. Suddenly daylight was blotted out, and he sensed that it was the enemy.

As the men of the South Wales Borders took cover, there was a burst of enemy fire.

The North-West Frontier Province (NWFP) lands six frontier districts of the Punjab compared to six tribal areas administered directly by the Government of India. On the other side of the NWFP was the buffer state of Afghanistan, separating the two empires, the Russian and the British.

The Durand Line, between Afghan territory and tribal areas which the British administered, bordered a belt of territory in which some tribes were vaguely regarded as British and others as Afghans; but neither were wholly subject to the authority of either power, though they were treated as British 'protected' persons. The tribes could thus play off the Amir of Afghanistan against the British, while the Amir intrigued with them to keep the British busy. People living in these areas were, therefore, very 'unsettled'.

The mountains of the NWFP were rocky and barren, with little vegetation and few trees. Waziristan, however, contained large tracts of deodar forest on its mountains, dominating slopes of open downs. It also contained scrub and small covered hills, together with bushes, stony plains and ravines, where the main tribe, the Mahsuds, had full scope to display their tactical talent. The heat in summer was searing, and the weather in winter icy cold. This drove its inhabitants to a life, half nomadic, forcing them to loot passing caravans. A man here looked at the world with suspicion and hostility. But fidelity within the group and between hosts and guests was a point of honour.

Life on the frontier had an immense appeal to the army. There were no long hours on an office desk and although there was the chance of a bullet and a good deal of discomfort, it was the life that most of us preferred. To the soldier, it presented an unrivalled training ground.

Our normal routine for four days, in the week, was to move out of camp at the crack of dawn, returning to camp before sunset. Our role was to picquet the hills on each side of the road along which our convoys were to pass.

These convoys carried food, ammunition and supplies for men holding garrison posts on route. Regularly, we were sniped at, by tribesmen holding the hilltops along our route.

We had, therefore, to clear these daring men out of their positions and hold these hilltops ourselves, until our convoys had passed. This required skill and courage. The mobility of the tribesmen on these hills was eye-opening to our men; as the tribesmen come down from the hillsides in a few seconds, like falling boulders, not running, but bounding. Occasionally, we had to carry out expeditions against the Mahsuds located in their strongholds. Our task was to surround and liquidate them. Their leader was the Faqir of Ipi, and he was actively hostile. We had to carry out again 'the forward policy' of former years and send troops into Mahsud country, where there was much fighting at the time. After Independence, the NWFP went to Pakistan.

On 23 January 1945, we were pulled out from Razmak and selected for jungle warfare training. We first went to Ranchi and then to Shillong, to train and fit ourselves into a formation, in preparation for Burma. I had been allowed to go to Burma, for a short tour, six months earlier, with a group of lieutenant colonels, among whom was Lt Col (the late Lt Gen.) Kulwant Singh, later GOC-in-C (General Officer Commanding-in-Chief), Western Command. Col Kulwant Singh was an enthusiastic officer but unconventional in many ways, sometimes becoming very impatient with others' views. As a result, he was inclined to 'rub people up the wrong way'. His views were always valuable; particularly on the Burma campaign, which we discussed many times and at length. All the officers were earmarked to take over commands of regiments intended for service in Burma. I went to the Arakan, where under Gen. Briggs, we learnt much about this special form of war, and where we also appreciated many and varied problems of an army in the jungle.

The British were very thorough in preparing a force for battle. They saw to it that their troops were always properly acclimatized, trained and equipped to meet the enemy on an equal or better footing. Our training on the North-West Frontier, our jungle warfare training at Ranchi and Shillong and above all my tour of the Arakan, under active service conditions, ahead of the regiment which I commanded, were of immense value. The soldier was systematically trained to hate his foe; for once the situation was handed over to the soldier, there was no question of the soldier making any attempt to win the enemy over by his generosity. Of course, civilization and culture always demanded that a correct code of conduct and behaviour be adhered to, and strong action was taken if a soldier failed in this aspect of his duty.

8

Missions Abroad (1945–47)

Historic events had been taking place in Burma where the Indian Army was being forced to withdraw from Rangoon towards Assam. So powerful had been the Japanese advance that they had, by the winter of 1943–44, reached the Indo–Burma border, and in 1944 they had out the lines of communication of the British IV Corps behind Imphal and laid siege to Kohima. For a short while, Japanese ships sank naval vessels, apparently at will, in the Bay of Bengal, and their aircraft raided Ceylon. Few realized how real was the Japanese threat to India. My youngest brother, Madhukar (now air vice marshall), who joined the Indian Air Force as a medical officer and had proceeded to Burma with No. 1 Squadron IAF as its chief medical officer, had a narrow escape. After the squadron was evacuated from Burma, he continued with an air force wing at Akyab, from where he and some others were evacuated, the day before its capture by the Japanese, arriving in Calcutta in pyjamas and one blanket.

The Japanese then tried to close in on Imphal but were prevented from doing so by Gen. (William) Slim of the XIV Corps—which had advanced from Imphal had crossed into Chindwin and Irrawaddy—had cleared the whole of

Burma of the Japanese. It was a brilliant recovery involving much courage, planning and hard fighting.

In July 1945, I was ordered to proceed with my battalion to Burma. We reached the lower stretches of Irrawaddy at Pegu, when news came on 6 August that the Americans had dropped the first atomic bomb on Hiroshima. Soon afterwards, Russia entered the war against Japan and on 9 August, the second atomic bomb was dropped on the port of Nagasaki. These events forced Japan to sign an unconditional surrender. The war against Japan now ended. On 29 August 1945, I was posted as second-in-command, brigade pool, in Burma, with the rank of colonel. This meant my leaving the battalion. But as the war was over, I looked forward to returning home. Instead, in November 1945, I was ordered to proceed to Germany, as second-in-command of the Indian Military Mission, which was to be set up in the British Zone in Berlin. I flew to Delhi, where I was briefed and proceeded thereafter to Berlin.

Berlin was in a sad state. The city had been heavily bombed and was in ruins. Debris and rubble were lying everywhere, and roads had to be cleared before vehicles could pass. We shared a portion of a building with military missions from other Commonwealth countries. Our role was to represent India in Germany as a military mission; to be later replaced by an embassy. The head of our mission was Brigadier D. Stuart, who had, at one time, been my commanding officer at Secunderabad. All the other members of the mission, with the sole exception of myself, were British officers of the Indian Army.

Our first task was to locate and contact Indian nationals, interned by the Nazis in Germany. This required us to extensively tour Germany in the British Zone, in our search for Indian soldiers and civilians. The devastation was so great that I hope never again to see a country in such a depressing state. The whole world would come to admire the courage of the German people who went about their day-to-day business under such tragic conditions. Their hard work and fortitude at this time had left with me a deep and lasting impression. Literally, nothing was left for them, yet they worked unceasingly, under the most heart-breaking conditions. Living in rubble, in a continental winter, they kept warm by such expedients as immersing their arms up to the elbows in cold water and rubbing them vigorously thereafter to encourage blood circulation.

A visit to Berchtesgaden was of historical interest. But the Nuremberg trials were of more importance and furnished quite a kaleidoscope of human emotions. Hitler and several other German leaders were already dead; but the twenty-two top-ranking Nazi survivors were tried on charges of waging war, violating the laws and customs of

war and committing crimes against humanity. Four of the
defendants were acquitted, but eighteen were found guilty
of one or more of the charges, seven of the eighteen were
imprisoned and eleven were sentenced to death. One of
these, Field Marshal Herman Goering managed to poison
himself. The other ten were hanged. During these trials,
whilst some of the accused pledged ignorance, avoided
responsibility or furnished excuses, Marshal Goering
unhesitatingly accepted the full blame for the total
Germany disaster and responsibility for all actions—a
very courageous step, worthy of a proud leader.

In our search for Indian nationals, we located among
other civilian nationals, Mr A.C.N. Nambiar, until recently
our envoy in Switzerland. We also found several bodies
of Indian soldiers killed and buried at Epinal and other
places. Our mission tried to establish fresh industrial and
trade relations with Germany, including arrangements for
the manufacture in India of the Volkswagen, the German
people's small car. But Germany was too badly crippled to
think of trade at that time.

During those eight months, while I was with the
mission, much was happening in India. The Quit India
movement was gathering momentum; so was Mr Jinnah's
demand for the creation of Pakistan. On 3 June 1947, it
was announced that India was to be partitioned, and the

Indian Army divided. I felt that my work was at home, and I applied for posting back to India. Two months later, my request was granted, and I was relieved in Berlin by Col Haauddin of Pakistan.

On my return to India on 2 October 1947, I was posted to Agra, as commandant of the Kumaon Regimental Centre. My work at the centre was concerned with the release of men wishing to return to civil life, and also with reorganization and training. My family joined me at Agra. Three months later, I again received orders to go out of India, this time to Japan, as part of the British Commonwealth Occupation Force.

Our duties in Japan were to protect Allied life and property and to ensure that directives relating to the occupation were carried out by the Japanese. In certain cases, it was found necessary to station small detachments at ferry terminals or railway junctions, to stop the illegal movement of controlled items. Throughout our stay in Japan, largely because of their loyalty to their emperor and their acceptance of the occupation, there was never any danger of an uprising. The greater danger was from the ever-recurring natural disasters, like typhoons and earthquakes. The Occupation Force, therefore, prepared a plan for each area which was to be put into operation the moment any warning of a natural calamity was received.

The Japanese police and civil authorities cooperated wholeheartedly with the occupation force in carrying out practices and putting plans into action. In addition to these duties, 268 Brigade Group, which I commanded, provided a guard battalion on rotation for the Imperial Palace in Tokyo. During the changing of the guard, the battalion band used to play martial music and attracted large crowds of spectators and batteries of cameras.

Though both these nations (Germany and Japan) had been defeated in battle, there was a vast difference in their conditions and the outlook of the two peoples.

In the former, Germany, destruction was absolute; but the people seemed to treat their condition as temporary, to be ameliorated by their efforts and not by external help. Their homes and institutions had been destroyed, their plant and equipment removed, their industrial production crippled and their economy reduced to ruins. The arbitrary partition of their country had separated friends and relatives, and there seemed little hope that Germany would ever rise again as a nation. Yet, the Germans were confident about their resurrection and strove to re-establish themselves, suffering untold privations and overcoming the deepest misery. They worked hard and unceasingly, giving fourteen hours of their working day, with little thought of tomorrow, often with meagre wages, and in some cases, without it; example, Krupp's for periods without wages at all.

Alfried Krupp Von Bohlen, the head of the Krupp family, was then in jail; but his men (Kruppianers) were so loyal to him and his family that they did not grudge working long hours without recompense until the firm was re-established. Krupp was known to be a fine man, sensitive, scrupulous to a degree, sympathetic and somewhat of a visionary, though now embittered because of his long years of imprisonment. It was loyalty and good management that brought back the firm to the coal and steel empire, it has almost become a legend in Germany. It is a pity that the fall in the coal market, the prices of steel and the policy not to dismiss any of his men have put Krupps now in such financial difficulties for his exports, that the government had imposed an Administrative Council on it. Krupp's financial difficulties have arisen mainly because of loyalty to his men, who he would not dispense with in this period of tight money. Had he lived, I have no doubt he would have maintained the Krupp family tradition and kept his family empire flourishing, as soon as the period of financial stringency was over. It was Rockefeller who said, 'Take away my machines, my business and my money; but leave me my men, and I will build bigger and better enterprises than I have today.' It was Krupp and Germany that actually did just that.

Those in Germany who could not find adequate facilities or scope for their employment at home migrated to other countries and set up establishments there, often from scratch. This was notably so in aircraft construction and design and missile development. Of course, there was a race between Russia and America for the scientists at Peenemunde; von Braun going to America, where his first few years were virtually wasted.

Dr Tank, the chief designer of the aircraft firm Focke-Wulf, eventually came to India, after a spell in Argentine. I had the good fortune to meet Dr Tank in the Hindustan Aircraft Factory at Bangalore where my brother (J.M.) was the managing director, and where he (Dr Tank) had earned the highest admiration for his patient, meticulous work and for his strict compliance to his code and discipline.

Dr Tank had a philosophy that all aircraft designers should be pilots themselves and be capable of testing their own designs. One can imagine the confidence that an aircraft would inspire, which had been test flown by the designer himself, and appreciate the knowledge of aircraft behaviour which test flights would give to the designer. Tank was an intrepid and dashing pilot himself who tested his own designs and was thus responsible for some original thinking. He gave a classic reply to a British aeronautical engineer who was expounding on the superiority of a certain British jet design: 'Have you ever flown one?' His design in India, the H.F.24, is a magnificent aircraft, well suited to our requirements and supersonic when provided with the right engine. Its versatility can be gauged from the fact that it was first tested as a glider without an engine. A British aircraft company was to have developed for us an engine, which we had purchased from them. We were going to manufacture under licence. But no British or continental firm participated in the acquisition of the developed engine, and the development costs became prohibitive for us. Egypt may develop, with our assistance, a suitable engine for this aircraft; and if it does, the venture will initiate a profitable developmental collaboration between two non-aligned nations, the first of its kind.

On the other hand, Japan did not suffer the massive destruction of war apart from Nagasaki and Hiroshima, where the destruction was nuclear and total. Its economic revival has also been spectacular, and it has maintained it in the face of unprecedented problems. Overpopulated and without adequate natural resources, Japan not only supplies its own population with unlimited quantities of consumer goods but manufactures for export at highly competitive prices. Importing raw materials, yet exporting the finished products at cheaper prices, is a feat few countries have been able to perform. Japan has been able to do it largely through discipline and hard work, which were abundantly apparent even during the period of occupation. We could emulate some of these habits, with an advantage.

All the available land in Japan along roads and railway lines or indeed anywhere, was intensively cultivated. Rotation of crops was achieved by careful planning and the quality improved with the cooperation from the agricultural department of the Imperial Japanese government. Both in Japan and in Germany, one became very conscious of the power of discipline, and the transformation it would achieve in the economic life of a nation. When one compares the ill efforts of indiscipline at home, in India, one feels sad that the object lessons received in Germany and Japan could not be available to moulders of public opinion in India. Japan had a unifying force in its emperor, and by its discipline has furnished an excelled example. Perhaps Germany, with its rise from utter destruction, has furnished a more convincing lesson for us, who have had such a sheltered life in India.

The Commonwealth forces, which occupied Japan after the war included contingents from Australia, Great Britain, New Zealand and India. India was represented by the British Indian Division under Maj. Gen. Dr (Punch) Cowan. It was composed of the British and one Indian brigade (268 Brigade) and divisional troops. The brigade had been specially selected as it had done excellent work in the Burma campaign.

The British–Indian Division was now dwindling in strength, owing to the departure of men being released from service. It was decided, therefore, that units of this division, still in Japan, should be formed into 268 Indian Infantry Brigade Group, under the command of an Indian officer. I was selected and soon after I took over command of this brigade, Maj. Gen. Cowan left Japan. Permission was now given for the families of Indian officers to visit Japan and ninety-six families in all arrived. These included my wife and my children, except my eldest son Satish, who was at Dehradun in a boarding school. Many of the Allied personnel and the Japanese met Indian families for the first time and were much impressed by the way they conducted themselves.

On 4 January 1947, I flew to Okayama (Japan) and took over command of the Indian Brigade Group with the rank of brigadier. On 15 August 1947, our first Independence Day was celebrated in Tokyo with great enthusiasm. The brigade took part in the parade at which the salute was taken by our ambassador, Sir Benegal Rama Rao. It was a proud moment, for this was the first occasion I had seen an Indian civilian take the salute of Indian troops at a ceremonial function abroad.

On 17 August, I received orders to proceed to Australia, as the Indian military representative at the Japanese Peace Conference, to be held in Canberra. These orders came after a decision had been taken in Delhi to withdraw all Indian troops from Japan. The withdrawal was necessitated in view of the constitutional changes and subsequent reorganization of the Indian armed forces. Our delegation at the Peace Conference was headed by our high commissioner in Australia, the late Dr R.P. Paranjpye, and included our ambassador in Japan, the late Sir Benegal Rama Rao. After the conference, I was posted to Madras to take over the Madras area, with the acting rank of Major General. Here, I worked closely with Lt Gen. Sir Archibald Nye, the Governor of Madras, a very able man.

9

Early Days of Independence

Much had happened in India in the meantime. India had been partitioned. The army had been divided on the general basis of 75 per cent to India and 25 per cent to Pakistan, the division being completed in the very brief period of two-and-a-half months. A joint Defence Council was formed to cover both the new countries and Field Marshal Sir Claude Auchinleck had become the supreme commander with administrative control over the two forces.

In July 1947, a month before the transfer of power, a Boundary Force came into being, with its headquarters at Jullundar [sic] and with the Fourth Indian Division as its nucleus, with Gen. Rees as its commander. The force was intended to maintain law and order, while the Boundary Commission proceeded with the task of demarcation.

It was anticipated that the Central Punjab, with a large area around the capital town of Lahore, would be the centre of the scene of disturbances. Approximately half the population of the area was Muslim, a fourth Hindu and a fifth part Sikh. But the Sikhs, by reason of their substantial landholdings, were scattered throughout the area in that part, which it appeared, would most likely fall to Pakistan.

At one time, there appeared to have been a hope that matters could be kept under control, but excesses through communal feelings on one side and retaliation on the other gradually mounted to a crescendo of excitement, and as the Partition's date approached, communal frenzy and fear gripped the population. Soon violence spread across the Central Punjab, resulting in bloodshed. The attacks on the civil population were barbarous in their ferocity and neither age nor gender appeared to matter. The Boundary Force, composed as it was of mixed forces belonging to both India and Pakistan, with officers including a number of British officers, could not serve the purpose for which it was set up; though it did in the early stages an excellent job. The majority of British officers felt that the communal feelings had surpassed any possibility of control that they themselves were too often suspected of taking the other side, and that there was no need for them to be involved at the risk of their own lives in a quarrel which was not theirs. The respective armies of the two countries appeared to be the sole stable elements in an otherwise uncontrollable situation, and their help to each other during the difficult period of partition (on both sides of the border) appeared to have set an example of brotherhood, which the civilian population could not emulate.

It is easy to condemn the killings, rioting, looting and the indiscipline, barbarous as they were. But, looking back after that period of stress, I am not at all sure that some of the manifestations were not the inevitable outcome of the idea behind the creation of the two countries. There was, on the one hand, a country to be carved out under the sectarian principles, and on the other, a non-sectarian state. The country to be partitioned had numerous religious and cultural minorities spread throughout its area, yet the aim was to produce a theocratic state, predominantly Muslim. How was the clean division to be made when the population was so heterogenous, and was composed of different religious groups in various pockets of the territory?

It was inevitable that the affected population would feel that minority pockets near the border should be 'persuaded' to leave; and that during this 'persuasion' it might be necessary to risk a few lives if other methods failed. But the repercussions of such 'persuasive' actions were not wholly foreseen. Retaliation was inevitable, as the reaction to the massacres at Rawalpindi in March 1947 proved.

Millions were affected directly, and it is difficult to imagine their feelings at the loss of their homeland and often their hard-accumulated earnings. But the loss of property and wealth were small matters compared to the loss of one's near and dear ones. My brother (J.M.), who was then in the unenviable position of the commissioner of the Border Division at the time of the Partition, told me of a soldier of the Boundary Force who had pleaded for permission to fire 'just one shot', in retaliation to the loss of his own family.

Discipline led him to make the request, and it prevailed with him even after the refusal of the request. But discipline is not one of the dominant characteristics of our civilian population.

A few days after Partition, it became clear that mass migrations were inevitable, and that this alone might prevent further bloodshed. But what was difficult to appreciate was the crude ferocity of rioting and murder. Such cruelty could not all be the outcome of retaliation, though ferocity must have increased on either side with each retaliation. Perhaps, the religious frenzy contributed more. It is unfortunate, therefore, that a solution for the division of the country with a sectarian state on the one hand and a non-sectarian on the other, had to be based on a religious principle.

Mass migrations were not, however, without incident or severe strain on the army, as the aftermath of the bloodshed had left its animosities. Even those leaving their homes and properties were attacked.

The first batch of refugees on road vehicles and on foot to be taken across to Pakistan, furnished a problem, as its route lay through the city of Amritsar, a Sikh holy city. In this town, one of the refugee parties from Pakistan had recently been attacked; and the night before the refugees were to cross, a large-scale attack was planned on the Muslim camp outside Amritsar, which was prevented only by the display of military force and the threat to use it. It had been prevented also because of the persuasiveness of the Deputy Commissioner Sardar Narinder Singh, Brigade Commander Brig. M.S. Chopra and Smt. Mridula Sarabai, who showed the utmost courage in the face of determination.

My brother (J.M.), who was the commissioner, received a threat of violence against his person in case any of the refugees were moved through Amritsar and got across the border. He became equally determined that the refugee column would go through unscathed. So, a conference debated till early morning the method of escorting the refugees through the city without bloodshed. Towards the end, Col M.S. Pathanan (now Lt Gen.) suggested the use of tanks. A plan was worked out with troops on the roads near the city and the tanks supporting the troops, to screen the refugees on the outer road. With the use of an observation aircraft to spot and report all collections of inimical groups, the column was led through unscathed. There was no molestation of refugees in Amritsar thereafter.

What helped considerably to put an end to all interferences with the refugee columns in the countryside, was a disaster caused by nature's intervention. Some refugees had camped on the banks of the dry bed of the River Bein near Jullundur. Unprecedented rains in the night in the hills and an unusual flood in Bein suddenly overtook the unfortunate group in the middle of the night, and before help could reach them, the camp was overwhelmed. Neighbouring villagers, which heard the cries in the middle of the night, came to the rescue, gave food, cloth and shelter to those who were on the periphery and could get out of the flood. But nothing substantial could be done for the others till the next day. The next day the river subsided as rapidly as it had risen and revealed the horror of families drowned in their efforts to move to places of safety. So rapidly had the flood risen that in some cases, complete families were trapped inside their carts together with their yoked oxen.

At Pompeii, one could see the preserved skeletons of those who attempted to escape the sudden overwhelming volcanic disaster, but one then felt that there surely must have been time enough to escape. But the position and posture of the families overtaken by the floods of the Bein made one realize how suddenly such calamities can trap and destroy human beings. The disaster evoked sympathy throughout the area, and there was little need for the army to guard any refugee columns in that area thereafter.

Just as there were examples of atrocities, there were fine examples of loyalty and humanity. Several families in the disturbed area continued to protect their Muslim friends and servants throughout the long disturbances and long after they were over. Young army officers, including my brother-in-law, now Lt Col K. Kochhar, crossed and re-crossed the disturbed areas accompanying the parties from one side to the other, in an effort to help those in distress. Civilian and police officials also frequently risked their lives without hope of reward or recognition, in the faith that their contribution might help to alleviate the situation and relieve some of the misery. My wife and I were much relieved when we received information in Madras that our son, Satish, who was then seven years old, had been safely evacuated from Lahore to Delhi at the height of this fury.

The partition of the army was an emergency operation made at express speed. Several units of the old Indian Army were of mixed composition and transfer of people according to their wishes was impossible. Again, a vaccum was caused by the withdrawal of British officers holding high appointments. These vacuums would have to be filled by Indian officers, even though they might not have been trained for the posts.

Because the subcontinent of India ceased to be a part of the British Army, and India and Pakistan were full members of the British Commonwealth, there was no longer any need for units of the British Army, the Royal Navy or the

Royal Air Force, to form part of the armed forces of the
two neighbouring states. The British forces stationed in
India had to, therefore, withdraw from the subcontinent.
An impressive ceremonial parade was held at Bombay,
which I attended as the representative of the Indian Army,
as the adjutant general. The parade was commanded by
Lt Col Prithipal Singh of the Sikh Regiment and was fully
representative of the Indian Army. The last British troops
in India, the first battalion of the Somerset Light Infantry,
ceremoniously passed through the Gateway of India with
the band playing 'Auld Lang Syne'. The long years of
dependence were over, and we were now on our own, fully
responsible for our country's defences.

There were thus two important tasks of reorganization
which fell on the AG's branch. In the first place, a large
number of British officers, who had left the country, had
to be replaced immediately. Military personnel who came
from and who opted for Pakistan and were serving side
by side with Indian soldiers were to be moved across
to their country. And units of the Indian states, which
became an integral part of India, were also taken over,
and men considered fit and suitable for further service
were absorbed in the Indian Army. All Gorkha regiments
had up to that time been officered exclusively by British
officers; and it had been assumed that they would all opt to

continue to serve under them. Surprisingly, six out of the ten Gorkha regiments opted for India, and they also had to be absorbed.

This reorganization in itself was a colossal task, but after attaining independence, we had to assume immediate responsibility for our country's defence, and two important constitutional changes took place in our defence set-up. First, the supreme command of the armed forces became vested in the President of India, while the responsibility for their administration and operational control passed from the British Commander-in-Chief, who held the dual role of the member for defence in the Viceroy's Executive Council and supreme commander of the three services, to the minister of defence, who became responsible to Parliament for all matters relating to the armed forces. Secondly, each service became autonomous under its own chief of staff.

It would be relevant to mention here that the role of India's armed forces up to and including Second World War, had been one of subordinate cooperation; and all policy was dictated from Whitehall. With Independence, and in keeping with the government's policy of non-alignment, the role now became primarily to defend India against external aggression; secondly, to assist the civil authority when required, particularly in time of national emergency or calamity, such as floods, famine etc.; and lastly, to help government in its aim of promoting peace by finding contingents to serve under the UN abroad.

Strategically, the Partition gave India additional frontiers, and Independence brought out the weakness of our defence against existing ones, in the absence of British support. These frontiers now bordered East Pakistan and West Pakistan. China, Nepal and Burma appeared much more vulnerable, because communications had been oriented to meet aggression (as in the past) from the north-west or the north-east. Railways and roads ran laterally from north-west to north-east and could be cut by any encroachment from the north. Up to that time, China had been disunited and weak, separated by a very forbidding country and by a buffer state, while the British might be something to be well respected. The position had now changed, and unless the Indian Army and its communication and logistic network could be reorganized and the army trained as a homogeneous and effective fighting force, there would be a vacuum south of the Himalayas.

But we were a peace-loving nation, with the people wedded to *ahimsa*, steeped in the belief that a peaceful attitude was a sufficient safeguard against any thought of aggression. As a matter of policy, we quickly expressed our close friendship with communist China, Nepal, Burma and Tibet; and we felt certain that, despite the necessity of Partition, and while deploring the communal frenzy that it evoked, the people of Pakistan and India were close kith and kin and would never dream of taking aggressive attitudes against each other.

So the role of defence was felt to be merely a posture, and most people thought that India would not, in the near future, be required to defend its frontiers. All that was necessary was to group the various units into a homogeneous whole, for employment in roles such as assistance to the civil administration and the UN.

Moreover, the attainment of Independence made us feel that the civil administration would not require that threat of force behind it, which had been a necessity during the time of the British—the rule was no longer alien and the civil administration would be 'government by the people for the people' with no reason to resort to the use of any force.

This type of thinking made itself manifest soon after we had embarked on the task of reorganization, which certainly kept us fully occupied in the early months. That task entailed developing the armed forces into a national force in character and outlook. Recruitment was thrown open to all classes and governed solely by merit and fitness. The distinction between martial and non-martial classes disappeared, though some units, like the Madras, Maratha and Sikh regiments, continued to retain their class names in the interest of tradition, discipline and efficiency.

JCOs replaced VCOs, and Hindi words of command were substituted for English. The army began to be reorganized on a mixed class confrontation, doing away with class regiments, regardless of origins, with the start being made with the guards regiments as an experimental measure.

But the general feeling grew that the army would not be required to defend our frontier or to be used in support of law and order. New India could do without the luxury of an army or perhaps make use of this disciplined force to assist the government in its developmental activities—in agriculture and similar operations. The fact that no group becomes an army without strict discipline and intensive field training was forgotten. Events a few years thereafter were to bring out the mistakes of that attitude; but it was gaining strength at that time, as I was soon to learn.

10

Kashmir Operations (1947–48)

History is often made through miscalculated or untimely political moves, and Kashmir is an outstanding example of such miscalculation and bad timing. At the time of Independence, Pakistan had in its favour, in Kashmir, an area adjacent to its territory, a ruler out of touch with his people and a preponderant Muslim population.

Pakistan had only to wait to win over the population, to influence the Maharaja to accede. But Partition was not Pakistan's moment for active steps in Kashmir, at a time when the population was loyal to Pandit Nehru for his self-sacrificing fight for their emancipation. It was then well known that Pandit Nehru had even been thrown into goal and banished by the Maharaja for his support to the people's struggle. Again, it was not a suitable occasion for a direct assault on Kashmir, at a time when the largest political party, under the dynamic leadership of Sheikh Abdullah, was advocating accession to India. Yet, presumably as a counsel of despair, knowing its case to be weak, and believing that the call to Jehad [sic] or 'holy war' would override these considerations, Pakistan selected this very period to launch determined attacks on isolated garrisons, forcing the state's forces to deploy in penny packets; and then, on 22 October 1947, to start a regular invasion of the state.

This invasion lost for Pakistan any claim which it may have professed to have had to Kashmir, and it also lost most of the religious support it might have previously received. Of course, Pakistan did, in the first instance, deny that the invasion was with her regular forces; but it later had to admit that fact to the UN face due to overwhelming evidence.

Several thousand tribesmen from the North-West Frontier, armed with rifles, machine guns and mortars, mounted on lorries, backed by regular forces, poured across the state frontier. They overran Muzaffarabad and Domel and pushed on towards Srinagar, along the motor road via Baramulla. Some Muslim troops of the state army joined the tribal raiders, while the majority of the local forces fought gallantly under the late Brig. Rajinder Singh; but they were overwhelmed. The invaders captured Baramulla within a few days, murdering and looting the Kashmiris, irrespective of caste, creed, age and sex. It became evident that their further advance to Srinagar was inevitable.

The Maharaja still continued to procrastinate; but when he saw that his capital was in imminent danger, he agreed to the people's desire to accede to India and asked India to rush aid for survival.

In the face of almost a fait accompli, and the knowledge that the Pakistan Army was committed, and because the agreement to help might mean involvement in war, the Indian cabinet met in an atmosphere of considerable tension and urgency. After a good deal of deliberation, it agreed to the Maharaja's and Sheikh Abdullah's request and ordered forces to be flown to Srinagar. As it transpired, these troops landed on 27 October 1947, at the only airport (south of Srinagar), when the airfield itself was being shelled; Lt Col D.R. Rai, leading the first wave of troops was killed on the airfield. The Maharaja's call for help came almost too late. Had the decision of the Indian cabinet to help Kashmir been made an hour later, our troops could not have landed. After landing, however, they were just able to stop the raiders on the outskirts of Srinagar. Our forces then built up their strength to a brigade group and moved to repel the raiders beyond Baramulla and Uri before the end of November. The Valley was made temporarily safe from the invaders.

In the meantime, the Southern Sector based in Jammu, had already seen large-scale fighting. Further, to the extreme north, the raiders had gained control over Gilgit through a coup supported by British officers and were besieging Skardu. It became necessary to send more troops, and another brigade group was therefore sent to Jammu, which started operating in the Naushera–Rajouri area in November. All Indian troops in Jammu and Kashmir were then placed under headquarters of Jammu and Kashmir Force commanded by the Major General (the late Lt Gen. Kalwant Singh).

50 Para Bde under the late Brig. Usman (he was killed in the fighting) fought gallantly in February 1948. Confronted by 15,000 raiders at Naushera, they successfully repulsed the attack, killing 2000 raiders.

Early in May 1958, the Jammu and Kashmir Force was divided into two. One was located in the Southern Sector and the other in the Valley. Sporadic fighting continued for some time, without tangible results on either side. In order to regain the initiative, Lt Gen. (later Gen.) K.M. Cariappa, who had taken over as army commander, Western Command, felt it necessary, because of the larger forces involved, to put these two sectors under one commander, responsible to him directly. In September 1948, I was selected for this task and named corps commander, V Corps, which consisted of 26 Infantry Division under the late Maj. Gen. Atma Singh with headquarters at Jammu, 19th Infantry Division under Maj. Gen. (the late Gen.) K.S. Thimayya with headquarters at Srinagar and an independent sub-area under Brig. (later Maj. Gen.) Jai Singh for securing the Lines of Communication (L of C).

These areas provided a wide variety of terrain and climate, including arctic conditions in the mountainous areas of Zoji La and Gurais, hilly terrain in Uri, jungles in Jhangar and plains in Jammu. They also contained the 260-mile-long Pathankot–Jammu–Srinagar Road, which was the lifeline of the troops, as well as of the civilian population. This lifeline was a hazardous route, crossing the Banihal pass at 9000 ft, which in winter was blocked by heavy snow. The Himalayan areas were also snow-clad and troops who had never before seen snow had to operate there.

The military situation in Jammu and Kashmir early in September 1948, when the command was unified, was far from satisfactory. Our garrisons at Leh and Poonch were isolated, and Pakistan was increasing her pressure.

Our L of C Jammu–Srinagar was threatened by infiltrations both from the east and from the west. Although Pakistan had launched no major attacks, our L of C Jammu–Naushehra was also very vulnerable. The threat to Jammu lay in its proximity to the Pakistan border, and to Naushera in the strong Pakistan build-up in the area of Bhimber–Sadabad. Fighting around Jhangar, Uri and Tithwal had been stabilized, and Pakistan had committed her regular troops in these areas supported by mountain and field guns. In the case of Uri, they had also brought up medium guns.

For India, the military situation in Kashmir had been adversely influenced by political considerations. Pakistan had no legal or moral right, in view of the expressed wishes of the people and its ruler, to operate with its army in Kashmir, whereas India did. India referred the matter to the UN, which set up the UN Commission on India and Pakistan (UNCIP), before which both parties came to an agreement to refrain from offensive action which was likely to aggravate the situation. Because of its strict adherence to this agreement, India was unable to use her air force in its primary role of isolating the battlefield by attacking Pakistan's supply and communications bases, or to attack Pakistan's installations on the Indian side of the border, inside Kashmir, such as Muzaffarabad and Mirpur, because of possible escalation. On the other hand, Pakistan made full use of the lull caused by the agreement to build its strength and supplement its forces in J&K territory, in such a manner that Poonch and Leh were systematically encircled. For Leh, we had an alternative means of communication via Manali; but the route was long and costly and only usable between June and October. Poonch, however, was so closely invested that our supply planes could not land there, while Pakistan constantly used her artillery, shells often falling amongst the refugees whom we had been giving shelter.

The general situation in September 1948, with Leh and Poonch in danger, was, therefore, militarily unsound; but was forced upon us—an example that arms are the servants of political policy. Pakistan continued to aggravate the situation, mustering greater and greater strength against the two isolated garrisons, preparing to defeat them in detail, failing which, starving them and the refugees into submission. The problem was whether we should evacuate these two garrisons or force a link-up.

The gaps in our line were from Baltal via Kargil to Leh and from Rajori to Poonch. Pram Baltal to Kargil (fifty miles), the track was snowbound throughout the winter, whereas from Kargil to Leh (150 miles), it was open throughout the year. Rajori to Poonch was only a distance of fifty miles, but this route ran over a series of high ranges and deep valleys with no tracks across them. If Kashmir was not allowed to be captured by Pakistan, we had to close these two gaps and link-up these garrisons. To achieve this end, we carried out two relief operations. I shall later describe those two operations: 'OP DUCK' (the name of which was afterwards changed to 'OP BISON', and 'OP EASY'), which led to the ceasefire.

For any operations, a reserve force is required to meet unforeseen contingencies. In these operations, the reserve had to be built up by making adjustments within the corps itself, for troops guarding other borders of India could not be spared. My divisional commanders readily cooperated with me and complied with all the calls I made on them for extra troops for reserves, from time to time, out of their limited resources. The approval of my plan of operations necessitated my flying frequently to Delhi, and it was only after many discussions and forceful insistence that I was able to obtain the agreement that once these plans were approved, the final decision to launch the operations or call them off, should rest with me as their progress would depend on local conditions which changed from time to time. In obtaining this agreement, I fully realized that had the operations failed, I would be replaced. But luck was on my side. I established my HQs in Udhampur and spent most of my time with formation HQs, taking part in the various operations, thus relieving my formation commanders of a great deal of individual responsibility.

Operation Duck (Later Operation Bison) (Link Up with Leh)

Between our forward position at Baltal and Pakistan's positions at Kargil lay a long stretch of fifty miles of mountainous territory, through which ran a single mule track, in a narrow winding valley, flanked by mountain peaks, rising to 17,000 ft. The Pakistan troops sitting in caves on these mountains, with positions carefully prepared and camouflaged, completely dominated the valley.

The task given to 77 Para Bde, commanded by the late Brig. K.L. Atal under the direction of Maj. Gen. (the late Gen.) K.S. Thimayya, was to break through this gap, capture Kargil and establish a link with Leh.

The first hurdle was the Zoji La pass (Blizzard Pass), a narrow 11,000-ft-high defile held by Pakistan. To secure this pass, our troops had to capture the heights on either side feature by feature and push the main force through the defile. Two attempts made in early September had failed.

The main reasons for these failures were that our artillery and aircraft could not go at Pakistan's troops in their carefully prepared positions; our infantry was not accustomed to operating in such difficult terrain at such very high altitudes; our troops had the greatest difficulty in climbing the snowy and slippery heights in the face of fire directed from well-sited defences; there was no room for our troops to manoeuvre so as to outflank these defences; and there was no special mountaineering equipment.

On taking over, I agreed that we might, with additional fire support, make another attempt based on the old plans. This also failed, and I reported this failure to HQs Western Command. The only signal in reply read, 'Change the name of operation to OP BISON and carry on', without any promise of additional troops!

The position now was that our three unsuccessful attempts had taken away the element of surprise, increased Pakistan's determination to fight and raised their morale. In addition, winter had set in. The plan had, therefore, to be revised to inject a fresh element of surprise into these operations; enable firepower of low trajectory weapons to be utilized, to force the intruders out of their bunkers; and discipline our troops to live and fight at great heights and in snow.

In spite of the disadvantages, I was determined that we should succeed and indicated my determination, to the officers conducting the operation. The reaction of one of the senior officers was that this fourth attempt at breaking through the Zoji La pass would also fail. In order to break this form of negative thinking, I asked him to put his point of view in writing.

This he hesitated to do, and I was able to proceed confidently with positive plans.

In order to support the infantry, in the initial 'breakthrough', tanks were suggested. But tanks had never before operated at 11,000 ft in snow, also they had to have firm ground to operate upon. In any case, it seemed almost impossible to bring tanks up to the pass secretly because the noise of their very movement makes their presence known. Further, in snowbound and hilly areas, tanks would be confined to narrow tracks where the formation of anti-tank defences against them would be simple. It was essential, therefore, that no breath of suspicion of the use of tanks should reach Pakistan.

As our first task was to get these tanks up to the pass secretly (a movement of 300 miles) without letting Pakistan know, I called the tank commander, Lt Col Rajinder Singh (Sparrow), later Major General, and Maj. Gen. Jai Singh, the officer commanding L of C area and set them to this task.

The idea of using tanks appealed to me because it would inject a fresh element of surprise into these operations and enable firepower of low-trajectory weapons to be utilized to force the intruders out of their bunkers by getting at them from the rear. For this, these intruders would be completely unprepared.

Tanks could be brought secretly up to the pass, by dismantling them and carrying them at night in trucks, without their turrets. They could then be reassembled close to the scene of operations, at Baltal.

During the later stages, movement at night would have to be undertaken without lights—a hazardous operation on the treacherous mountain road, from Baltal to the Zoji La pass.

Coordination could be affected by night reconnaissance and briefing on the sand model. But we did not know how our light tanks (Stuarts) would behave on the snow and ice, which lay on the pass and the valley beyond. Any knowledge which could be obtained by ground reconnaissance and by questioning local people about the state of the ground could not disclose the information that tanks may be used. If the terrain could not hold tanks, or if any anti-tank weapons were brought up against them, the tanks with their crews would have to be written off. The possible loss of the tanks and the bogging down of the operation had to be weighed against the effect on the morale of the material success of the operation which would have cleared the whole of Ladakh and made Srinagar more secure.

The tanks were brought down to Baltal by road, which was hastily improved, by our engineers working at night. Lt Col Rajinder Singh and Maj. Gen. Jai Singh and their officers and men deserve the highest praise for their courage and enthusiasm, and for the way in which the tanks were brought up to the pass after assembling them at Baltal. In spite of the fact that news travels quickly in the valley, such was the secrecy of these operations that even our own forward troops did not know of the presence of these tanks until they had reached Baltal.

The country between Zoji La and Kargil afforded the intruders full opportunity to fall back, when defeated, on to a series of natural defensive positions. It was important, therefore, that our initial thrust should be so powerful that it would prevent the Pakistan troops from falling back gradually and delaying us from one position to another. Again, it was important that an adequate reserve of supplies and transport be collected at Baltal for immediate use as soon as the initial thrust had succeeded, and an organization be ready to construct a jeep track behind the advancing column as the Infantry Brigade moved forward. We appreciated here the superb work of our engineers, who worked unceasingly for days to get their jobs done.

Our operations had to be completed before the heavy fall of snow. Originally, we decided to commence the operation on 20 October, but bad weather and snow prevented movement, and the Zoji La pass would become impossible to negotiate in December. I fixed, therefore, 1 November as the last day for launching the operation and stocking across the Zoji La, which after that date would have been difficult, because it required at least a month to stock up the garrison for six months—the period during which the Zoji La pass would be snow-clad.

On the morning of 1 November, I was again present at advance headquarters near the Zoji La pass. Though the weather had cleared somewhat there still was light fall of snow, also the air reconnaissance on which we had depended so much, could not be made available. This was bad news, but we were promised air support immediately after the weather cleared. In the meanwhile, we were we to launch the attack without 'air' knowing that, if the weather went further against us and the snowfall continued, our attacking forces would be bogged down.

I took a calculated risk and gave orders to launch the attack, accompanying the attacking formation. The light tanks moved forward, crossing the Zoji La pass, stepping on to 'No Man's Land' in the Gumri plain. They then forged ahead through snowdrifts, glaciers, mountain streams and over boulders, to reach the rear base of the hill held by Pakistan, who opened a barrage of fire. This ricocheted harmlessly off the tank armour. Even then, Pakistan would not believe that these were real tanks!

The tank guns now came into action and systematically destroyed some twenty-five bunkers. Behind the light tanks, the infantry moved forward without much opposition. Pakistan troops were surprised and demoralized, and the attack was successful. The Zoji La defile was negotiated, and the Gumri Plain was captured before nightfall. Kargil fell on 23 November, and the link-up was successfully achieved. I felt happy that the operation was a success.

The Zoji La breakthrough did not have the heavy air and artillery cover, which had become a normal phase of the last war, nor was it accompanied by the high percentage of casualties, which occur in modern battles. For example, at the Battle of Keren (Ethiopia) in March

1941, the Rajputana Rifles, in capturing a feature known as Hogg's back, lost over 50 per cent of its strength. The 2nd Battalion Maratha Light Infantry also suffered heavy losses capturing a hill referred to as 'Flat Top' (one platoon having only three men left). The Zoji La operation, during which we lost forty and 100 were wounded, proved that modern weapons (like tanks) could be used at altitudes greater than they had ever previously been used. After the initial breakthrough, 77 Para Bde was seriously held up only once, at Pindras, fourteen miles from Zoji La, where we were forced to halt to enable our administrative tail and light tanks to catch up. Pindras was a strong natural defensive position, in a broad and winding valley, where the hills on each side were not so precipitous as at Zoji La. We learnt here that the quickest way of maintaining the momentum of the advance was to push through boldly with our infantry on a broader front and not rely on tank support to neutralize enemy defences.

Thus, because we appreciated early, that surprise and speed were the essence of the operation, we achieved satisfactory results and forced Pakistan, in a matter of three weeks, to withdraw fifty miles, from a series of strongly held natural defensive positions.

Some further lessons learnt during the course of these operations were:

Reconnaissance

The scope of reconnaissance was limited because ground maps of a larger scale were not available and also because of restrictions on air flights due to high hills and bad weather. However, we appreciated that the most suitable time for air reconnaissance was soon after fall of snow, when Pakistan troops in clearing snow off their bunkers, automatically disclosed their positions. Commanders also relied on information through local knowledge and sent out fighting patrols at night.

Supporting Fire

We found that the intruders, holding properly camouflaged positions in caves on hillsides, could stand any amount of artillery and air bombardment; but weapons with a flat trajectory such as .30 Browning of the Stuart tanks, were effective when they could be brought up to correct positions. The direct fire of the 37 mm gun of the Stuart tank was also very effective in destroying bunkers.

Maintenance

The problem of maintenance would have been severe enough whilst operating 300 miles from our base, and with the L of C passing over the Banihal pass, closed for part of the winter. But it was rendered more difficult by the alpine nature of the climate and the great heights at which the operation took place.

Strange things happen at great heights. The slightest movement exhausts energy, water takes hours to boil and troops halted on the line of march freeze quickly and find difficulty to move again. The only antidote is rest and acclimatization which require time and which we could not afford; for heavy snowfall threatened, and the momentum of the attack had to be maintained.

Construction of a Jeep track behind the advancing troops and stocking up Forward Maintenance Areas for the winter were also problems requiring the greatest skill and experience. We had not only to provide supplies, ammunition and POL (petroleum, oil and lubricants), but also to provide special winter equipment and firewood.

There literally was no firewood anywhere from Baltal to Kargil. Consequently, every bit of our requirement for the whole force had to be carried either by men or by local ponies. So great was the need for firewood that all wooden telegraph posts in the line of advance from Zoji La to Kargil were quickly being removed by the advancing troops to supplement their rations, for warmth was then the greatest need of the soldier. Little did I realize that an ill-disciplined soldier would even go to the extent of burning his blanket for a few minutes warmth today, though this might result in his freezing tomorrow. At the same time, with disciplined troops, the impossible was made possible; for example, when a Gorkha picquet of 11 ORS at 16,000 ft which could not be withdrawn due to sudden heavy snow, survived for six weeks on two weeks' rations.

Weather

Weather was most important, particularly because we required air support. Twice we had to postpone operations because of adverse weather. On the third occasion, on 1 November, the weather turned out dull and intensely cold, with light snowfall and poor visibility. We had to then decide whether we should launch the operation without air support or cancel it altogether, because even 1 November was late enough. Without air support, on the initial day of the thrust, we would be losing two of our greatest assets, namely firepower and morale, and this would slow down our advance. As our tanks and infantry were poised for attack, we decided to take the risk and launch the operation on that day, without air support (such alternatives will frequently confront commanders, and it is well to think of them in the planning stage).

A week or so after the capture of Kargil, there was a heavy and sudden fall of snow. This snowfall buried 230 of our vehicles between Baltal and Dras, of which fifty were swept off the road by severe avalanches. The precaution taken by our drivers in using an anti-freeze mixture and the efficiency of our IEME (Indian Electrical/Mechanical Engineers) enabled us to recover all the vehicles and make 180 of them quickly road-worthy.

Health

The problems which faced us were intense cold, frostbite, trench feet, headaches, insomnia, breathlessness and anoxia. We believed that effective prevention was a matter of discipline. Figures show that, although our troops had on many occasions waded through ice-cold water, our frostbite casualties were few. To quote an incident, an officer during operations, swam a 50/70 yards in a frozen river without any ill effects. Where, however, our officers were unable to enforce orders regarding changing of boots, using dry socks and rubbing feet daily with mineral jelly, owing to the rapidity of our advance after Zoji La, and where our mule column was cut off for many days by heavy snowfall in early December, our frostbite casualties increased from fifty to 500, and fourteen of our gallant soldiers permanently lost the use of some limb. I cannot, therefore, overemphasize the importance of discipline, as a preventive measure against frostbite.

Morale

Our previous unsuccessful attempts to break through at Zoji La had lowered the morale of our troops. Commanders built up morale by intensive training under local conditions and by tackling human problems. However, the final morale boost came with success—that panacea for all mental ills. At Pindras also it became clear that man is the first weapon of war, and on his fighting qualities and understanding of his problems depend so much in battle.

Air Support

As in Burma, maintenance by air once again played a vital role. When six months' stocks of 77 Para Bde (rations, clothing and equipment) were buried under snow during stocking, the formation had to be maintained entirely by air for that period. In fact, this had to be accomplished by air drops, as at that time, there was no airfield at Kargil.

OP EASY (Link-up with Poonch)

This operation was ironically named 'OP EASY', because of its complexity in planning.

It was in striking contrast to the operation for the link-up with Leh. Whereas the latter was conducted by a brigade group along a valley, the former, namely the

Poonch operation, which involved a division, had to traverse a series of high ranges and deep valleys. The high ranges were held by Pakistan infiltrators in considerable strength and the capture of these ranges by day, presented an extremely difficult task.

Though carried out at much lower heights (5000–7000 ft as against 10,000 to 14,000 ft), the operation was equally strenuous. The absence of roads entailed complete dependence on animal and porter transport and on supply drops, until jeep and mule tracks could be constructed. The three to one numerical superiority enjoyed by the infiltrators, the advantage they gained from the series of traverse ranges, could not be overcome by direct assault. So, we decided to divert their attention from our main objective: Poonch.

Nature of Operation

The operation was mounted with two brigades and two battalion columns under the command of Brig. (the late Maj. Gen.) Yadunath Singh, under the general direction of the late Maj. Gen. Atma Singh.

To secure the L of C, 268 Infantry Brigade, under the command of Brig. Harbhajan Singh, captured Pir Badesar on 15 October. The brigade was supplied by air and ordered to demonstrate towards Kotli, giving the impression that an advance to Kotli was intended.

The 19 Infantry Brigade was then moved secretly to Rajaori to join 5 Infantry Brigade. As a further feint, ad hoc brigade at Rajaori was ordered to demonstrate towards Thana Mandi. In the meantime, 5 Infantry Brigade, under Brig. (later Lt Gen.) Umrao Singh, captured Pir Kalewa.

On 8 November, the 5th, 19th and Rajaori Brigades made a three-pronged attack towards Kotli and Bhimber Gali. On the capture of Ramgarh Fort and Bhimber Gali, the Rajaori Brigade was left to protect the L of C and construct a 15 cwt (hundredweight) track to allow field guns and light tanks to come up to Bhimber Gali. The necessity of having field guns well forward in the advance was fully appreciated. So, guns were moved forward not only by constructing tracks rapidly behind the advancing troops, but also by moving them into suitable positions by light tanks and bulldozers, and sometimes, on to a hit of high ground, by hand.

On 13 November, the 5th and 19th Infantry Brigades were pushed from Bhimber Gali on a two-pronged advance towards Mendhar, again giving the impression that the main thrust was directed towards Kotli. 5 Infantry Brigade on the east took all its objectives, but 19 Infantry Brigade on the west encountered stiff opposition, in an area south of Mendhar, known as the 'Gold Feature'.

As the primary object of the operation was to establish a link with Poonch, a battalion of 19 Infantry Brigade was left to contain the opposing forces, while the rest of the brigade was switched secretly to the east and joined up with the 5th Infantry Brigade, thereby reinforcing success.

On 22 November, 5 Infantry Brigade relieved Poonch; 19 Infantry Brigade thereupon passed through and attacked the Gold Feature from the rear, thus securing the whole of the Mendhar Valley.

This operation delivered lessons in the value of deception, the proper use of night operations and the importance of maintaining communications.

Deception

The key to the success of this operation was deception. If the intention to link-up with Poonch had been apparent at an early stage, the operation would probably have failed, as Pakistan had sufficient force at its disposal to hold us— in a country which was admirably suited for defence. By demonstrating towards Pir Badesar, Kotli and Pir Kalewa and by carrying out deceptive air drops, we led him to believe that Kotli was our objective and made it disperse its forces.

Night Operations

As the country was traversed by a series of high ranges held by Pakistan in strength, we could not conduct operations during daylight without accepting heavy casualties. We, therefore, selected vulnerable points in this position and captured them by series of night advances from one firm base to another. The success of such operations depended on intensive night training before the operations commenced; and thorough and secret ground reconnaissance by commanders and by as many troops as possible.

Maintenance of the Line of Communication

Owing to the complete absence of roads, the commanders had to rely on local animal transport and porters. The latter were not dependable, but housing and feeding them and their animals and prompt payments increased their reliability and made their employment more effective. Work was often done quicker and cooperation was rendered easier by appointing a leader amongst the porters themselves. The lack of roads also aggravated our problem of the evacuation of casualties and forced us to employ porters as stretcher-bearers. Sometimes the carriage from the Regimental Aid Post to Jeep-head took twenty-four hours; consequently, we found it necessary to move our surgical teams well forward of the jeep head. This was good for morale. Construction of roads to take jeeps, and later 15 EWTs was a major problem.

The capacity of these roads was limited and subject to the slightest change in the weather. This limited capacity called for the strictest convoy discipline and block timings. In spite of this discipline, efficient staff work and regular supply drops from the air, the strain on our maintenance was severe. It, therefore, became necessary to sort out essential and non-essential personnel in forward areas and withdraw the non-essentials to the base, thus decreasing the demand on our logistics.

By now, Pakistani forces had received severe blows from our successes in Operation Bison and Operation Easy and were generally withdrawing. But orders were received to stop further movement forward until the United Nations reached an amicable settlement. The reason for these orders appeared to be that Gen. (Sir Francis Robert Roy) Bucher, C-in-C India and Gen. (Douglas David) Gracey, C-in-C Pakistan, being connected with each other by phone, had calculated that any further move forward by us in the Poonch–Rajaori sector would bring the main Pakistan Army into direct conflict with the Indian Army. This possibility, the two C-in-C felt, should be avoided at all costs, as both dominions were in the Commonwealth. This was an unfortunate directive to our army, as some of us in the field felt that as the Pakistan forces were on the run, we could have driven them out of Kashmir further. Stopping Indian troops from going forward afforded Pakistan an opportunity of putting its house in order. For it was able to establish his HQs 2nd Army at Rawalpindi. This force was to have three divisions, two under command and 9 Infantry Division at Kahuta and Muzaffarabad and 7 Infantry Division in the Sialkot–Jhelum areas, in support. It had become clear that Pakistan wanted to launch an all-out effort to stage a comeback in Kashmir.

It was in pursuance of its offensive intentions that Pakistan started shelling the Southern Defences of Naushera–Sadabad area and Beripattan Bridge on 14 December 1948, by bringing into action two batteries of heavy anti-aircraft and some medium guns. With these sixty artillery pieces, or so, it fired over 3000 shells, within twenty-four hours. It also made an unsuccessful attempt to assault our positions south of Naushera.

Our troops held on firmly and gave not an inch of ground. But the heavy shelling continued till 17 December, which disrupted our communications. On the last day, the Beripattan Bridge, which was under direct observation, received a hit from an eighty lb shell and was seriously damaged. The engineers, however, had already constructed an alternative road to Naushera via Sunderbani, and this route was put into use forthwith.

The Pakistan guns to be silenced were in the Kabutargal area, with an observation post at Pt 3754. We planned to capture Kalidhar and Pt 3754 from the east.

On 20–21 December, 80 Infantry Brigade's officiating commander, Lt Col (later Brig.) Y.S. Moghe, under the direct command of V Corps, carried out this operation. The 2 Kashmir Infantry formed a firm base at Pt 3807, while the 7/2 Punjab attacked Pt 3754. The troops swam across the Manawar Tawi River in winter floods, climbed over precipitous terrain and launched a silent attack after thirty strenuous hours. This was a feat of endurance that completely surprised Pakistan forces. A hand-to-hand fight took place, the position was stabilized and Pakistan guns silenced.

By the end of 1948, both countries agreed to a ceasefire, and I was named leader of the Indian delegation, which negotiated in July 1949, the demarcation of the ceasefire line in Jammu and Kashmir. The other members of the delegation were Maj. Gen. (the late Gen.) K.S. Thimayya and Brigadier S.H.F.J. (now Gen.) Manekshaw. Shri H.M. Patel and Shri Vishnu Sahay attended the negotiations as observers. The Pakistan delegation was led by Maj. Gen. Cawthorn and included Maj. Gen. (now Field Marshal) Ayub Khan. We had our meetings at Karachi.

The ceasefire agreement was officially ratified by the two Commanders-in-Chief at their meeting in Delhi on

15 January 1949, where the following arrangements were agreed to:

a. There should be no advance forward from positions held on 1 January 1949.

b. Commanders of the opposing forces in Marol, Jhangar, Uri and Tithwal would meet and carry out local adjustments.

c. Prisoners of war of the regular army, state forces and Azad forces would be exchanged on a man-for-man basis. On completion of this exchange, the raiders and Pathans in civil custody would be repatriated in exchange for the remaining state force prisoners of war.

d. Isolated Pakistan garrisons along the Kishenganga may be maintained by Pakistan by air.

Thus ended fourteen months of fighting in Kashmir, which has been the story of a limited war, because India was anxious that the area of conflict should not be extended. In fact, these operations on our side were restricted to Jammu and Kashmir alone. At the same time, we had to keep other troops deployed on the Punjab and Rajasthan borders as a deterrent against a possible extension of the war by Pakistan.

I shall conclude by saying that in Jammu and Kashmir, we had achieved much largely due to our better discipline and training. We must remember that this was the first time in decades that Indian soldiers under their own commanders were fighting for their country and not for a foreign power. There had been a myth that Indian soldiers could only fight under British officers. This myth was busted.

I have always had great faith in the fighting qualities of our soldiers, and it was reaffirmed in this campaign, where I was much impressed by the way our young commanding officers, with only seven and eight years of service, planned and coordinated operations, and handled troops under battle conditions. It was no surprise to me, therefore, that similar leadership qualities were displayed in the Indo–Pakistan conflict in September 1965. I am confident that India will always be proud of the fighting qualities of its soldiers and the leadership qualities of its young officers.

11

Senior Appointments in the Army

Soon after the agreement on the ceasefire line in Jammu and Kashmir, the enormous responsibility of becoming the first Indian Commander-in-Chief (C-in-C) of the army devolved on Gen. K.M. Cariappa on 15 January 1949, with Lt Gen. D. Russell, the senior-most British officer present in India, as his military adviser. There was tremendous enthusiasm amongst all ranks on his appointment, because it was the first time in the history of the new Indian Army that we had an Indian chief. Indeed, some of us had never before served under an Indian commander. Pride appears to lurk in every human heart and is evoked in a variety of ways. To us soldiers, it was a matter of deep pride that we had our own Commander-in-Chief, and we felt that we had at last our 'own Army'—a factual symbolization of our 'Independence'.

Gen. Cariappa, affectionately known as Kipper, had a very human and likeable personality; British in his mannerisms and speech, and yet, much in him was Indian. As the first C-in-C of the army, he was an important figure in the country. So, what he said in public or to the press was carefully noted and reported. Despite this, he preferred to be frank and outspoken. Sometimes, his spontaneous utterances got him into difficulties with the authorities and caused embarrassment to his colleagues. Having to step into the shoes of leaders like Field Marshal (John Eyre) Auchinleck, Gen. Cariappa had to maintain some of the tradition and the pomp of a British C-in-C, and at the same time maintain close contact with the Indian soldier. This he did remarkably well, for he had a glamorous personality and was a great patriot. He threw himself wholeheartedly and enthusiastically into the work of creating the new national army—strong, disciplined and loyal to the country.

Kipper's Hindi was unique, but he spoke it so charmingly that we liked to hear him talk. On one occasion, he spoke a few words to a soldier in Hindi, to which the soldier replied in more colloquial Hindi, 'Sir, I do not understand English.' However, I sometimes wonder whether Kipper's utterances, some of which appeared outrageous at the time, were intended to provoke a dialogue or were knowingly shed in good humour. On another occasion, he enquired in Hindi from a young officer's wife, returning from her honeymoon, where they had gone. Alas there was no word in Hindi for honeymoon; so, Kipper coined one: 'Shahad Ki Chand'.

Thus, 15 January became an important day in the history of the Indian Army and was named Army Day. A convention was set for the army's C-in-C to take salute and address troops at a ceremonial parade in Delhi cantonment on this day, in which representatives from the several units of the army took part.

Before Independence, the British had located their forces largely in the North-West Frontier, where the population was aggressive, and had placed garrisons near towns or near capitals of states having Indian rulers. There was no need for independent India to garrison its states after their masterly integration was accomplished by Sardar Patel. There was also little need to guard the large towns, except as a measure of internal security. Pakistan's attack on Kashmir and its belligerent attitude towards India, however, necessitated the guarding of our new frontiers with that country. It was recognized that East Pakistan was not only less belligerent, but after Gandhiji's visit to Bengal it was more amicably disposed towards us. Our other neighbour China had at that time (1947) not embarked on the surreptitious encroachment of our territory but were loud in proclaiming their brotherhood to India.

After Independence, India was divided into three commands—Southern, Eastern and Western. Southern Command, apart from the long sea borders had a major portion of the Rajasthan border, as well as several important training institutions like the Staff College. Eastern Command became operationally active later, on the involvement of East Pakistan in the hate campaign against us, development of Chinese design across the vast Himalayan border and the growth of the Naga and the Mizo movements. Western Command included the states of Jammu and Kashmir, East Punjab and a portion of Rajasthan which had long and active borders with West Pakistan.

Three new army commanders were appointed, Lt Gen. (the late Gen.) Rajendra Singhji as GOC-in-C Southern Command, Gen. Nathu Singh took over Eastern Command, and I was appointed GOC-in-C Western Command with headquarters at New Delhi. The three army commanders, whom Gen. Cariappa generously referred to as his 'props', were responsible directly to the C-in-C for matters relating to operations, discipline, training and administration. The C-in-C held army commander's conferences twice a year, at which the principal staff officers, heads of services, director of Military Intelligence, director of Military Training, director of Military Operations and the Military Secretary also participated. These conferences proved extremely useful in the reorganization and the creation of our new army.

The long and active border with West Pakistan kept me busy, and I had to regularly visit the border areas and keep in close touch with the troops. Establishing Western

Command entailed the creation of a new command to exclude the areas which had gone to Pakistan, working out defences in depth, the siting of permanent stations for new formations, and organization for a revised logistic set-up. Further, it necessitated establishing new areas (Jullundur and Delhi), which were to liaise with the civil authorities.

Owing to its heavy duties on the West Pakistan border, Western Command contained most of the field formations of our army. Consequently, it had training responsibilities in addition to operational commitments. I, therefore, held numerous exercises in the field, and on sand models, to train infantry and armoured commanders in handling their formations. I was fortunate to have capable officers on my staff, among whom were Brig. (later Maj. Gen.) U.C. Dubey, Brig. (now Lt Gen.) Harbaksh Singh and Brig. (later Maj. Gen.) R.N. Nehra—all of them men of high ability and thorough loyalty.

The headquarters of Western Command was in New Delhi, which was not an ideal situation for an active operational command, as it became too involved with army headquarters and the Centre. I suggested that the operational command should move to Delhi Cantonment nearby, which would have all the advantages of being close to the authorities concerned and yet be at the same time, not physically part of them.

On 15 January 1953, Lt Gen. Rajendra Singh (Reggie) was promoted C-in-C in place of Gen. Cariappa, who had retired and had been appointed Indian high commissioner in Australia, and I was transferred to Southern Command to take over from him. Lt Gen. D. Russell, the military adviser, also retired and there was now no longer a senior British officer in the Indian Army.

Southern Command had few operational problems, but I was confronted for the first time with the question which cropped up in one form or another during the rest of my army career: 'Why should India have a standing army when it was a peace-loving nation, which also was not aligned with any of the great powers and might get involved in war?' In Western Command, there was a large land border with Pakistan, with which had we been involved somewhat antagonistically both in the civil strife at Partition and in the defence of Kashmir. The north-western people had also the background of invasions suffered by their forefathers. But in the south, Pakistan was far away, and the strife and hatred evoked by the civil disturbances at the time of Partition had hardly any repercussions. To the civil population and authorities, the army was a body apart from which to keep aloof; and at the same time, a luxury, as it appeared to have no specific task in times of peace and in the face of our non-aligned foreign policy.

Similar concepts, I was to learn later, pervaded Delhi, the headquarters of government, and the seat of our legislature, but in a somewhat modified form. Here the question was: 'Why could we not reduce the size of our army or use it for civilian development work when we had no enemies, and intended to be at peace with all the world?'

These two questions in their various forms fogged clear thinking, often prevented careful planning of the future organization of the armed forces and interfered in training. These questions kept cropping up not only in planning discussions but often in social exchanges with civilian officials and personages who influenced public opinion; also, they did nothing to improve relations between the civil and the military.

One of our primary tasks, therefore, apart from the normal duties associated with a command, was one of education and moulding of public opinion and the promotion of a better understanding between the army and the civil. In this task, I had the valuable assistance of the Brigadier General Staff (BGS), Brig. (later Lt Gen.) Moti Sagar.

How were we to explain the danger of a power vacuum—(the desires and hopes it evokes in the neighbourhood and the urge to fill it?)—particularly when the explanation meant discussion of a political subject, where a soldier must surely tread with caution? The need of an army was unobtrusively brought out. In talks to civil audiences and press representatives, I explained the organizational structure of the army, showing how it was trained for battle, and the reasons for continuous military training year after year. Quite a few people felt that army effort should be devoted to the production of food. It was made clear that the army was not a static organization, for there was a major turnover of personnel each year. New equipment and new weapons had to be constantly introduced, and new techniques for their use had to be learnt. There was also the problem of training in different kinds of terrain i.e., jungle, desert, mountain and plains. All this required time to ensure that the army became an efficient arm of government and worked as a team; little time could, therefore, be devoted to other tasks. But the army was always ready to assist in an emergency.

Perhaps these informal talks were useful in helping to remove some of the opinions against the maintenance of a standing army. Such concepts were understandable because the army was the largest non-productive organization in the country and was regarded in some circles as a legacy of British Imperialism. Further, the maintenance of a standing army was expensive and reduced considerably the money required for our economic plans. The fact that our army had saved Kashmir and was readily available to help the country in times of natural calamities, such as floods and famines, gave confidence to the people that the maintenance of an impartial and efficient standing army was necessary. Later events have made us realize that army training is vital for our existence, a fact that is not apparent during times of peace. The Chinese war found us unprepared, with soldiers from the plains attempting to fight at 17,000 and 18,000 ft, against troops which had been seasoned at these heights. Troops unacclimatized to such heights can barely move without extreme exhaustion and suffer from anoxia. Our troops had also little conception of Chinese tactics. Exercises in logistics for a war of this kind had not been carried out, with the result that our jawans spent many bitter nights at sub-zero temperatures in summer clothing, without even blankets. To have fought in such conditions was little short of heroic.

The Pakistan war, on the other hand, amply bore out the effectiveness of adequate training. Pakistan had been supplied with superior equipment, which if used effectively could have disabled our air arm and destroyed our forces. It is largely the training and effective use of our weapons and their efficient maintenance by the common soldier or airmen that negatived the superior Pakistan aircraft and destroyed the vast proportion of their admittedly superior armour. We will have to remember in future that Pakistan has now learnt the value of adequate and intensive training and will use its equipment for more effective purposes

Morale plays an important part in any organization; but it plays a vital part in the army. In a service organization, disintegration can set in very rapidly if 'morale' is low. Much has been written and spoken about 'morale', but to build and maintain morale in an organization as big as the Western Command required a great deal of vigilance when individual unit commanders played an important part. But an equally large part was also played by the conditions of service. To bring this factor 'home' to the authorities who controlled the finances of the defence forces was a major task and remained so during my entire service, though I must admit that some finance officials were very far-sighted and allocated funds in a masterly way. Getting adequate funds for housing was always a problem, because the shortage of accommodation was so vast we had lost three-quarters of our cantonments to Pakistan, and at the one time, had retained three-quarters of the army. The absence of accommodation for families often became a most demoralizing factor.

Another factor was leave. Leave is granted to provide officers and jawans with a break from work. In the army, if a man is lucky, he can get one or even two months leave in a year. I have always tried to avail myself of such leave, but it was often refused or cut short, especially in times of emergency.

On one such occasion, I proceeded on two months' leave to a small hill station, Chakrata, in the UP (United Province). On the third day of our stay, we arranged to go on a picnic, in which our friends were first to gather at our house. Half an hour before the agreed time, a note came to my wife saying that one of the couples we had invited was unable to come, as the husband's leave had been cancelled, and he had to return to duty that afternoon.

My wife asked me why our army authorities could not plan leaves in a better way. She felt that it was unfair for a young officer to spend so much money and effort in bringing his wife, family or old parents for a holiday, only to be recalled soon afterwards. My wife, after unloading her frustration on her husband, returned to her picnic basket. In about five minutes, I followed her with the inevitable pink telegram in my hand, which I handed over to her. She was astonished to see the telegram, and then immediately started packing, for I had also been recalled. Instead of staying over with us for the picnic, our friends were able to say goodbye.

In less than four hours, the house was shut, and everything was packed—curtains, carpets, cutlery, crockery, utensils, stores, pictures, bedding, servants and even the dog.

When we boarded our transport and started our downhill journey, my wife remarked, 'It has taken me four hours to pack. The next time you are recalled, I shall do so in half that time.' This is, I suppose, the best way for an army wife to accept life in the army.

We generally went to quiet places for our holidays; sometimes to a small hill station like Chakrata, near Dehradun. This was to enable us to have a real change from the hectic life of a big city and also devote time and attention to the children. We used to interest children in nature studies, such as birdwatching. This sometimes resulted in us having to climb trees to see birds' nests, which the children had discovered. It also afforded them considerable amusement to see us climbing trees, especially when they had to help us up part way.

Some of our holidays were spent on '*shikar*', and if we were lucky, on a tiger shoot. This is a sport still available in India, but only to those who have the good fortune to be able to arrange it and afford it. We, of course, could not afford this luxury, but on a few rare occasions were fortunate enough to be invited to join friends.

A tiger shoot is a thrilling experience, especially if one has the good fortune to see the tiger in its native habitat. One of my tiger shoots took place in Kotah state, with His Highness whom we had known for some time—a cultured man and a generous host. I would say that today he is also one of the most knowledgeable shikaris in India. Apart from being a good shot himself, he has filmed wildlife and produced excellent films depicting jungle life. Her Highness of Kotah is a talented lady with a charming personality. She has travelled widely, accompanying her husband on his tours abroad. All the members of the Kotah family are good shots.

On this occasion, we drove from Gwalior to join their Highnesses holidaying at Thana, a small village 100 miles or so from Kotah, with a tiger jungle around. Each guest, with his family, was housed in a large tent with a screened veranda all around it. Though it was summer and the heat intense, the camp arrangements were perfect. Maj. Gen. (now Lt Gen.) Thorat and Maj. Gen. (now Lt Gen.) Bahadur Singh, whose home is at Kotah, were also at the party.

We arrived in camp late in the evening and after a bath and change, joined their Highnesses at an open-air dinner. Life in the camp was informal and friendly. We went to sleep with high hopes, and after breakfast the next day, waited in expectation of news. Time passed slowly. My children, who had accompanied me, were highly excited and enquired frequently when they were going to see the tiger. At last, the news came of a kill, but we could go to the place of the kill only early next morning. So, that day we organized a general beat around the camp, rode elephants and sat on *machans* (small platforms on trees constructed as points of vantage).

We were called very early the following morning. The place of the kill was an hour's drive from the camp, which we reached just as the sun was rising. The car engines were switched off and we approached the place silently on foot. We were on the edge of the north bank of a river, which overlooked the far bank as well as the river. The far bank was sparsely covered, with stunted trees and little foliage. The riverbed itself was green and with tall shady trees and shrubs, near which were pools of water. It was an ideal tiger country.

We all were cautioned to be careful not to make a noise. We noticed a viewpoint nearby, a stone wall with a thatch cover. While others were asked to sit quietly where they were, I was taken to this viewpoint. There, through a gap in the wall, I saw a magnificent sight. Next to a pool of water and under a tree, in the open, was the tiger feeding on the kill, quite oblivious of us. There was dead silence, except for the occasional caw of a crow perched on a nearby tree. From the distance came the call of a solitary peacock.

Despite this silence, the tiger was alert and from time to time would survey the surroundings suspiciously. I watched this unusual sight for some time through binoculars.

The valley was deep, and the tiger seemed far away from us. I calculated that it would have to be a long shot, and I debated the consequences in my mind. However, as I was not to shoot till later, I enjoyed for the moment watching every movement of the tiger, a truly magnificent sight. We then gave an opportunity to others in the party to see the tiger, who was still quite unaware of the happenings on the other bank. When we all had a good look, His Highness signalled to me to get ready to shoot.

We moved up to the viewpoint. I was flanked by His Highness on one side and Maj. Gen. Bahadur Singh on the other. These were cover guns, in case the tiger was not killed in the first shot. A tiger is a king in the jungle when he is unmolested; and only a tiger when he is disturbed. When wounded, he is ferocious and invariably attacks on sight—elephant, man or vehicle. A plaque in one of the reserve forests commemorates the leap of a wounded tiger, to grip a eighteen-ft-high machan, and tigers have been reported as charging 100 yards after being shot through a vital part.

It is for this reason that the government prohibits tiger shooting with bullets of less stopping power than a .375 magnum, and experienced hunters will invariably have supporting guns in case the first shot does not kill, to avoid the necessity of a long, hazardous and nerve-wracking follow-up after a wounded animal.

I raised my rifle, took a deep breath, aimed carefully and pressed the trigger. The tiger dropped, but to my surprise, was gone in an instant. I had obviously hit it, but the shot was not fatal. The tiger was immediately seen dragging himself a little upstream. Bahadur immediately rolled it over dead with a shoulder shot. Everyone by now was looking over the wall and talking excitedly.

This was not my first experience of tiger hunting. I had sat on a machan on a pale moonlight night over a 'kill' with my colonel when I was attached to a British regiment. Though all kinds of strange jungle noises kept our nerves on edge, the tiger did not appear. It was getting late and very cold, and we decided to return. But this meant a descent from the tree into the jungle, and a journey on foot of three jungle furlongs to the cart track, with the tiger prowling near the kill. So, I was quite prepared to let my commanding officer descend first and lead the way. To my discomfiture, he said, 'After you, my boy.' I explained to him my respect for rank and age and attempted to hint that rank and ago should set precedence. However, orders are orders!

12

The Chief of the Army Staff

Service in Southern Command had given me an indication of the civil reaction to a standing army in peacetime; and allowed me to appreciate the changes required in a democratic set-up. The Commander-in-Chief of the forces would naturally be the President, the senior-most appointment in the army would be the chief of staff, and the county would think in terms of a smaller and a truly national army. Yet, the chief of staff had to plan five to ten years ahead, with the knowledge that a weak and demilitarized nation would inevitably invite attacks on its long and extended borders. The very length and nature of the land border, comprising as it did, many miles of the lofty Himalayas, the thickly populated areas of Punjab and Bengal, the vast expanses of the Rajasthan desert, the water-logged areas of the Rann of Kutch and the inaccessible areas of Assam connected with the rest of India the only by a narrow strip, furnished problems even for a large army.

When I took over as the Chief of the Army Staff in 1955, the size of the army was in the region of 4,50,000. Efforts were being made to reduce it at the rate of 10,000 men per year until the figure of 1,50,000 was reached. This figure of 1,50,000 was not based on any study of our defence requirements, though a detailed survey was necessary to determine what size the army would be for the foreseeable future. Unfortunately, at that time, the government being attuned to peace and non-aligned at attitude, felt that the army was an expensive luxury and should be turned to part-time police, given labour force duties or employed to grow more food. The public had obviously not grasped the complications of modern-day soldiering, and it was difficult to make understand that military training was a serious matter, requiring a full-time schedule of work.

However, after numerous discussions, the government, taking a more realistic view of problems regarding the security of the country, accepted a 3,00,000-force plan and agreed not to include tasks which could better be accomplished by police or a labour force. The acceptance by the government of the strength of 3,00,000 combatants for the army in the foreseeable future also meant a large increase in the substantive rank structure, a large intake of cadets at the Military College, and with it all, a firm commitment to build the necessary accommodation and the agreement to procure equipment on a long term basis. These matters naturally involved greater expenditure, and the money could only be diverted for defence from other welfare commitments. The decision to accept a 3,00,000 force was taken in the teeth of strong opposition, which continued for some time even after indications of possible attacks on the border had become apparent. It was taken reluctantly even though there were indications that our borders were not being treated as sacrosanct.

There were other consequences arising out of the fact that the army had come into hands, with an Indian chief of staff and not a Commander-in-Chief, at its head. First, during the British regime, the army was looked upon as a mercenary force paid to enforce British authority; whereas it was not a people's army, maintained to secure its borders. But the people's view of the soldier still continued to be influenced by its previous role. As an example, in Trivandrum, no civilian had any contact whatsoever with the Gorkha soldiers stationed there. In fact, these soldiers were looked upon as foreigners and shunned. This was not an isolated case, such attitudes had to change, and the soldiers accepted as the citizens' own. Again, to maintain the army as an efficient force, it had to recruit the best material, and deep-seated prejudices in the minds of our young people about joining the forces had to be eradicated. I was personally very glad when my eldest son Satish selected the army as his career; and I continued to encourage families to think in terms of having at least one son in our national army. Then again, if the prejudices against an army career were to go, the army man had to

have something to look forward to 'on his retirement'—
as he retired earlier than his civilian counterpart. To give
his life in war and to retire early in peace, in emoluments
less than his contemporaries and friends, did not induce a
man to select an army career. It was, therefore, necessary
to find alternative employment for army personnel on
retirement. So, I was happy when the government accepted
the principle of employing selected retired army officers as
civilian administrators and managers.

My immediate task, however, lay in reorganizing and
housing the army and equipping it with suitable weapons
also in intensifying training. Because of the US arms aid to
Pakistan and its build-up, plans for reorganization and re-
equipment of the army began to take quicker shape. The
aim was to increase the army's hitting power. Housing also
became a problem; for not only had 75 per cent of the army
come to India on Partition, but, as the greater portion of
the army was previously stationed on the North-West
Frontier of India, most of the cantonments went to Pakistan.
In addition, the army had to be regrouped to man India's
frontiers. New cantonments had, therefore, to be built.

I conducted several exercises in the field for training
formation commanders, and for practising their operational
schemes; and introduced the method of study on sand
models of modern military problems, such as the effect
of nuclear strikes on troops in the field, and the necessity

of integrating defence science research with armed force practices. We also invited our scientific adviser to be a member of our advisory staff, with responsibility for part of the execution of the exercise.

The need for leavening the concepts of the armed forces with the development of modern science has been recognized all over the world; but there is no consensus on the method of accomplishing this, at a time when such rapid advances are taking place in the field of science. We have the advantage of the experience of the British government during Churchill's regime and of their advice. The armed forces in Britain have also seen the consequences of relying too much on the advice of an expert who did not carry the ministry with him, and they have equally suffered from an administrator who had not been in touch with the latest technical developments. We, who have limited technical personnel and limited resources, could take advantage of the reports of the Plowden Committee or the Bhabha Committee, for example, and also of the experience of other governments. If our adviser is a pure scientist, then we should help him with the administrative set-up. If he is an administrator–scientist, out of touch with recent developments, then we should give him the necessary experts.

There is, however, a great deal of knowledge and new thinking in our own forces of which we may not be taking full advantage of, because of too strict an adherence to set procedures. One of our senior generals has said that he would not encourage free expression of views in the army council as it might lead to indiscipline. To me, it seems that the objective of the council is lost if the free expression of views is not encouraged, and we are only limited to the views expressed by the top man.

We do not seem to have gained from the experience of the failure of the German war potential during the last World War. Much of this potential was critically reduced by Allied bombing. The programme of bomber construction by the United States and Britain was known to the German High Command. The failure of the first British bombing attack on Heligoland Light had proved the superiority of the fighter. Yet the high command continued to give low priority to the lighter programme till as late as October 1944, a year before defeat, when it was too late. A jet fighter, superior to Allied fighters, had been developed by Messerschmitt, but it was not introduced as such. However, it turned into a high-speed bomber. British and American successes in radar and accurate bombing pointed at increased value of radar techniques. Yet, reliance continued to be placed on unaimed bombing, and science and industry were not given the necessary encouragements. In Germany, it might almost be said that the method of conducting the war was a classic example of the failure to coordinate the efforts of science and industry. There was no combined services staff, who could exchange ideas with the leaders of science and industry. The departmental method of organization prevented communication of military requirements to science and industry on the one hand, and the knowledge of technical advances and industrial developments to military commanders on the other.

Our resources being limited, it is all the more necessary for us to learn from the experience of others. To fail to take advantage of the knowledge and experience of our scientists and technicians, and at the same time discourage the upsurge of new ideas would be, to my mind, the height of folly.

In obtaining agreement to our plans, we were fortunate in the ready understanding of the defence minister, under when I served. Dr Katju was always patient and appreciated the problems of coordination, particularly with other ministries and departments in government. A jawan on seeing Dr Katju's hearing aid, remarked, 'Dr Katju listened to you with one ear, while "listening-in" to the prime minister (through his hearing aid) with the other.'

During 1955, I visited the UK and USA. In the UK, I attended the War Office's indoor exercise ('Onward'), for which several senior Commonwealth general officers, including General Ayub Khan from Pakistan, were present.

The exercise conducted by UK 8s CIGS Marshal Sir John Farding was in two parts, which bore no relation to each other.

Part I of the exercise dealt with problems connected with the integration of Commonwealth forces working together in a foreign theatre. It was thought that an exercise of such a nature would be of use, particularly at a time when Commonwealth countries were planning to take over some of the defence burdens so far borne by the British alone; for example, in Malaya where the British, Australian and New Zealand forces were considering joint operations. Such discussions would also, it was thought, be useful for countries participating in NATO and Middle East defence organizations.

Problems connected with integration do not naturally concern us directly, but the discussions were interesting. Lessons drawn from the recent experience of integration of the Commonwealth forces made the subject more practical. Speaking generally, Commonwealth commanders are not prepared to surrender their right of trial over their own personnel, so it was thought sounder to let discipline continue to remain the responsibility of each Commonwealth component under its own service code. Subjects such as pay, leave and length of service in the theatre of operations were also matters in which the

Commonwealth countries considered that integration was inadvisable.

Part II of the exercise was conducted on a cloth model and was designed to study the defence and major counter-attack under conditions of nuclear warfare. The primary objective of the exercise was to ascertain what was the best organization for such an operation. The question was whether the armoured regiment should form part of the basis organization of the brigade, or whether the armour should be grouped under it. Our own brigade commander, within the Infantry Division, gave rise to considerable discussion. The majority opinion, however, was for grouping the armoured regiment under a brigade commander and not locating it within the basic organization of an Infantry Brigade. In the experimental armoured battalion, it was interesting to note that the commander directly commanded four armed regiments: one-armed C. Regt, one infantry, one Mod. Regt (SP) (Modern Regiment [Self-Propelled]) and one-armed Transport Squadran (Tpt Sqn), without an intermediate Brigade Headquarters (Bde Hqs).

In his closing address, the CIGS said that America was important to the Commonwealth as the Commonwealth was to America. He also stressed the importance of studying the technical side of modern warfare and made a plea for closer cooperation between Commonwealth countries, which were independent states covering and equal partners of a big family.

While in London, I met our own officers—Gracie, Lord Mountbatten, Gen. (Frank) Messervy and Field Marshal Alexander—stationed there and several others, unconnected with the exercise, including the plan.

In the USA, I was given the opportunity to visit the important military installations, such as the Amercian Cadet Academy at West Point, the Command and General Staff College at Leavenworth in Kansas and the Centre of Army Aviation in Alabama.

Cadets at West Point have to live up to a high code of conduct. Even at meals, first-year cadets (Plebes) are expected to eat at attention. The honour system for maintaining discipline is used, and the punishment for law breachers is prompt and severe. The decision to expel a cadet, who had violated discipline, is left with the commandant (known as the superintendent) with the rank of lieutenant general, who is advised by senior cadets as well as officers on the staff, and political pressure does not influence the decision. Cadets who graduate from the academy receive a BSc degree, and the accent is on academics, particularly in physics. The standard of mathematics and science is high. Civil professors of the academy wear uniform, without the badges of rank to indicate that despite the special attention being paid to the study of purely non-military subjects, the atmosphere of the college is military. Of the 2500 cadets of the academy, who incidentally feed together in one large dining hall, there were few foreign students, and perhaps not more than three black students. During the course, cadets are taken around to visit numerous other military installations. West Point is a college well-run and produces the right type of officers; but our college at Kharakvasla [sic] is equally good and has the added advantage—unlike West Point, it integrates the basic training of the three services.

The ceremonial arrangements in the USA were well organized: a formal reception at the airport by officials representing the chief of staff, Gen. Maxwell Taylor; an Honour Guard at the airport with a salute of seventeen guards (apparently standard practice for all full generals); introduction to officials of the military and state departments; a formal one to Gen. Maxwell Taylor at the Pentagon (where I was presented with the 'Legion of Merit' in the degree of commander); the laying of a wreath on the grave of an 'unknown soldier' where the national anthem of both countries was played; and a formal reception by our ambassador, Shri G.L. Metha, an eminent economist and a man of great character, were the main feature of the official ceremonies.

Not only was the ceremonial impressive, but I was fortunate, on my fourteen-day tour of the USA, to obtain a representative comprehensive view of the military organization of the country. Though our reception was most cordial, I found at Washington some caution in our discussion with senior officers of the Pentagon. It was pleasant to hear how well students from our own army had done in the course they had attended in the USA, and what a good impression they had left. I was surprised, however, by the largeness of the number of Pakistani, Iranian and Turkish officers being sent to the USA for training.

Black troops had been well integrated into the US Army as a whole; and, as far as work was concerned, there appeared to be no difference between 'white' and 'coloured'. But black personnel were not seen at the officers' clubs; and during off duty, they seemed to live a life apart.

The American Army is largely short service, the maximum term of enlistment for the other ranks being two years. Officers emphasized the difficulty of obtaining both efficiency and cohesion with the short service terms and admired our long service system. Side effects of these short service terms were visible in the low standard of drill in general and slackness, though the turnout was good.

At home, an association with the Chief of Staff Committee convinced me that our top defence organization was not the most suitable for our country. Today, the chief of staff of the three services, from the Chief of Staff Committee, presides in rotation. It usually meets once a week to coordinate inter-service matters relating to administration and training and to discuss problems referred to it by the defence minister. As the chairman is fully occupied with his own service, he is not able to devote his full time to inter-service and higher service defence problems; and the civil secretariat cannot also give full time or its best experience or accept the responsibility for the effective solutions of such problems. The chairman should be a full-time officer, selected as the best from the three services, given the highest rank and thereafter relieved of the necessity of loyalty to his own service. This would enable him to devote all his efforts to inter-service and higher defence problems, without responsibility for the administration of his own service, which would be left to the service chief concerned. In this way, he would render expert military advice to the defence minister, whose primary aim is to ensure the security of the country. The defence policy has to be based on an analytical and local appraisal of the likely threats to our security. In a politically stable state, internal threats are generally minor. In our own case, such threats would come as a result of shortages, famine, inflation etc., resulting in upheaval. The military consequences of such a situation must be appreciated by the top defence organization.

But the major threat to our security will always be from external sources. To appreciate such threats, the top defence organization should analyse the national interests of the countries, which are capable of threatening our security and deduce from them what is likely to be their foreign, economic and military policies. It must also be appreciated that even if a country has hostile intentions, it may lack the capacity to implement such intentions. For this reason, the capacity of the country to commit aggression must also be analysed. This would include her industrial base, technological know-how, economic capacity, communications, raw materials, availabilities etc. Had we been giving thought to such problems, we would have been more aware of the Chinese threat and its magnitude.

Again, such analyses must be carried out only by teams highly competent and not preoccupied with other routine duties. As the whole purpose is to analyse information from the defence point of view, such an organization must be headed by a very senior serving military man, with a lifetime background of military appreciation. It is he who should be selected as the chairman of the chiefs of defence staff. He must be served by the requisite number of teams, mainly consisting of service personnel with foreign office associations, who would be capable of examining the strategic factors affecting our defence.

It would follow that until we create such a top defence organization, our defence policy cannot be related to the actual situation that the country is likely to face from time to time, and therefore, the size, shape and organization of our defence forces cannot also be formed on the desired lines.

Some against the proposal to create a post of chief of defence staff generally put forward the view that India was no longer likely to be called upon to fight in distant overseas threats. But surely planning the protection of our borders, especially when they include sea and land frontiers, islands and promontories, has to be as thorough and detailed as planning for action in a distant theatre. India has also to be prepared to fight on two battle fronts, east and west, at the same time and while doing so, has to ensure the security of the state from within—for which a sufficient force has to be kept in reserve intact, apart from the tactical reserve. The chief of the defence staff would have to take an overall view of the defence position and would frequently have to go against the view of a single service. But the overall view would certainly be better than the present system of compromise. In war, there can be no compromise.

I understand that the proposal to have an independent chief of defence staff has been mooted time and again, subsequent to my retirement from the army, and that it has been regularly turned down despite its merits.

Again, it would make for speedier and more efficient disposal of work, if the service headquarters is integrated with the Civil Secretariat to form the top defence organization. The defence minister would continue to bear the overall charge and responsibility, while the civil services would be able to play a more effective role in the formation of policy, with constant and regular advice from military experts. As regards problems of each separate service, the minister could be advised by a council composed not only of civil and service officers but perhaps also of important non-officials having specialized knowledge.

Our borders present special problems because, in some parts, they are undermarked; for example, in the inaccessible portions of the Himalayas; and in some, they are shifting, as when the boundary follows rivers which change their courses, e.g. in Punjab. Our long and undefined borders, stretching hundreds of miles, have involved us in disputes, which some neighbours occasionally feel can be settled only by forcible occupation. We are, therefore, compelled to face the prospect of having to drive intruders from isolated areas. At the same time, the armed forces are called upon to intervene when tribes, or other internal groups, decide to assert their independence by armed conflict. Such types of warfare are in effect 'limited wars'; where the armed forces cannot use their full resources. In such conflicts, the armed forces are also limited in the areas fought over (e.g. when they are not permitted to go on beyond certain boundaries); or they are restricted by the nature of the conflict (e.g. in the trouble with the Nagas, where the government instructions are to win them over). Such restrictions are not normal for an army at war because they curtail the initiative and the effectiveness of the army and confuse the army's aim, which should be total destruction of the enemy's forces.

Limited wars are a highly specialized form of warfare. This is because a neighbour, who gets too aggressive, has to be promptly driven out and cannot be permitted to continue in illegal occupation, pending the longer strategic approach required in a general war. They are specialized also when a militant group gets too powerful and has to be contained without disturbing the remaining peace-abiding population.

As we are likely to be involved willy-nilly in limited wars increasingly on our borders, let us take advantage of others' experience of such fighting and appreciate that, because we have the resources, courage and determination to carry out a general war, it does not follow that we have the capability of undertaking 'limited wars'. The success of the latter operation depends on superior resources being mobilized quickly at a particular place and time, to respond instantaneously to aggression. This is what the British did on the North-West Frontier of India, where such operations continued over a long period. They had adopted their weapons, in the way of machine guns, armoured cars and even aeroplanes, especially for this type of fighting. The training of their soldiers was also highly specialized, suited to the particular operational requirement. However, the fact remains that, despite these advantages, it took many years of fighting to defeat the Fakir of Ipi.

It would appear that we might perhaps take such steps as the following, to enable us to fight limited wars:

a. Place in the hands of our young men, who have to handle them, the weapons and equipment best suited for the purpose. For example, where the country is woody and mountainous, a semi-automatic weapon is preferable as it gives quicker firepower for close-range action without the necessity of carrying vast quantities of ammunition. In the Vietnam War, the mortar has proved to be the most-effective weapon.

b. Give the local authorities the power to take adequate action quickly, without long references and explanations to the government.

c. Encourage the active support of the local population. This can be furthered by giving the local population in the areas in which they live, some stake and, therefore, a reason for defending their areas against hostile non-Indians.

d. Where the population in border areas is thin, or their loyalty questionable, induct in these areas strong and patriotic people from other parts of India. As an example, people all over India have been anxious to settle in Kashmir; but because of local feelings, this has not been possible, with the result that Kashmiris alone (with, of course, the backing of our security forces) have had to stand up against Pakistani infiltrators these last eighteen years. It must be universally accepted that India belongs to Indians as a whole, and not that portions of the country belong to one particular community.

e. Refrain from the temptation of deploying our regular army on the border too early. For early deployment destroys the army's characteristics and surprise value, and takes away its initiative, preventing its utilization on grounds of its own choosing.

f. Establish more paramilitary forces, like the Assam Rifles, to help in looking after border areas.

I was fortunate in my health and was categorized 'fit for active service', at the time of retirement, which was now drawing near. So, I gathered my children one day and explained that when I retired, I would naturally have to give up the many privileges attached to my office. My youngest son, Ravi, who was then seven years of age, was quite affected by the loss of the privilege of flying a flag on our car. He reacted quickly by making a paper flag for his bicycle and using it all around the neighbourhood.

My long service in the army has convinced me that the soldier's loyalty to his service, his love for his country and his constant sacrifice, deserve adequate recognition from his fellow countrymen. I have a profound respect for the common man of India, from whose stock the soldier comes and believe that 'every soldier is a citizen and every citizen a soldier'.

No one hates war more deeply than the soldier, who specializes in the arts and instruments of war; and perhaps, no one is more keenly conscious of its senselessness. Every intelligent person shares the hope that another world war will be avoided. But while tensions remain and there is a lack of international agreement on control of atomic energy, there is little room for complacency. Serious efforts, therefore, must continue to be made, at least to limit atomic tests, for it is difficult to foresee what suicidal developments may come about in the next few years. As a soldier, I go further and say that human life is so fragile that, as between ordinary bombs and atomic bombs, the individual has little to choose. The threat of conventional weapons or even short-range ballistic missiles, casts a shadow over men's hearts. I believe, therefore, that the dominating effort should be for the preservation of peace, rather than for preparation for war; and that it is not atomic weapons alone, but war itself that should be outlawed; for victory poses more questions that it answers.

13

The Administrative
Staff College of India

Just before I retired from the army, Dr John Matthai, chairman of the Court of Governors of the Administrative Staff College and a former finance minister of the Government of India, invited me to be the first principal of the Administrative Staff College. I pondered over this invitation for some time because the concept of an administrative college was new to me. Of course, the armed forces keep training their officers at various stages, sending them on courses and to staff colleges and expecting them at intervals even to take examinations. This is part of the system for orienting officers to new branches of work, and part of the officer development programme. In civil administration, however, such training was never contemplated except at the initial level. The United States had set the example of training business administrators and manager and had introduced courses for executives and others in business and industry, to be undertaken after some years of service. But in administration, the idea of training those already well-established in their various fields was somewhat new, particularly to India.

The participants of courses in the Administrative Staff College were to be mature men experienced in their own fields, and presumably well conversant with administration. Such participants would not have become accustomed to attending courses at different intervals in their careers as officers of the armed forces, and it would be something new to these mature men. How would they react to being sent to school again? How many of them would be able to settle down again to intensive reading? How would they discipline themselves to be resident members of a group . . . away from their homes and families, away from their recreations and normal social life? Why should they accept the discipline of a regimented life, to which they were not accustomed, and which they might feel they were now too old to undergo? What would they learn from this new form of teaching?

The first principal would be expected to establish the college and set the tone; and he would be expected to impart this 'training' to experienced civil administrators. It would be a real challenge for a soldier to head this civilian institution. I accepted the assignment.

The first task was to understand the system to be introduced, and I was accordingly deputed to spend six weeks in attendance at a course in Henley, the British Administrative Staff College, and the model on which the Hyderabad Staff College was to be based. Various methods of instruction were used by management and business administration schools which catered to working personnel in the US. Probably, the most famous is the Harvard 'Case' method. Here, a business problem was formulated, based on facts gleaned from actual happenings, and a case was prepared. This case was presented to the group of participants and discussed—each participant is required to study the case, comment on it and suggest a 'solution'. This solution was critically discussed by his colleagues and defended by him. The object of the exercise, however, was not to 'find a solution', but to bring out the principles involved and underline the causes. Other 'schools' adopted other methods of instruction, such as lectures or seminars by the Massachusetts Institute of Technology or discussion groups. The lecture and seminar method certainly collected material and made available to the participant the knowledge of the professor. It did not necessarily ensure that the participant imbibed their knowledge. Columbia University, on the other hand, adopted a mixture of systems, using lectures, seminars, group discussions and the case study method to enable participants to imbibe information and ideas.

The Henley System, however, seemed to be quite novel. The participants were selected from different spheres of activity, governmental, business, professional etc., and were split into groups of ten, each group being representative of a different interest, and the group being as heterogeneous as possible. A 'Paper' prepared by the school was then discussed by the group of ten (called Syndicate) with its own, selected by rotation without any interference from the college's directing staff (one of whom sat in on the Syndicate) except for very rare guidance. The Syndicate then trial to reach a consensus or a group solution.

The Syndicate method subjected mature men to the impact of the experience of others in similar conditions and forced them to defend or modify their own views and systems of work.

Important persons such as Shri Sanjiva Reddi, Shri T.T. Krishnamachari, Shri M.C. Chagla, Shri Ashok Mehta, Shri Humayun Kabir, Shri J.R.D. Tata, Prof. Thackar, Dr P.S. Lokanathan, Shri P.L. Tandon and Shri Jehangir Gandhi were contacted. A number of them gave valuable advice and active support.

These influential personalities were very helpful in the sale of the syndicate idea to government and business houses, in obtaining their initial and continued support for an experiment, of the success of which in India we ourselves were not certain, as this was to be the first institution of its kind in the east.

Dr John Matthai was an effective chairman with a clear vision and sound common sense. He was pleasant to work with and had a keen sense of humour. He had been a minister for some considerable time in the central government. When he was minister of railways, he told a story against him, at a time when there was much criticism in the public regarding the slow running of trains. A railway employee decided to commit suicide by lying down across the rails, at a time when the fast mail train was due. He waited patiently for the train's approach; he waited and he waited, and he eventually died of starvation.

In establishing the college, we had the unique and general support of both the central and state governments and numerous private sector organizations. The Government of India made a non-recurring grant of Rs 7 lakh for capital works and equipment and a recurring annual grant of Rs 3 lakh for the first three years. The Ministry of Education also agreed to give an interest-free loan of Rs 9 lakh for the building programme. The support given by large and small industrial enterprises in the public and private sectors was equally generous. The problem of establishing the college included the challenge of starting an institution from scratch, a problem that few of us had so far to face. Apart from the sale of the syndicate idea, a building had to be found which could be suitably modified, to furnish not only the syndicate rooms and the Central Assembly Hall but also the individual residential quarters for the fifty or so participants coming from all walks of life. It had to provide catering and other facilities, including recreational activities. The building work was entrusted to architects, engineers and contractors in Hyderabad, and the work was completed well in time for the start of the first session at the college on 6 December 1956.

This building plan was intended to facilitate the proper functioning of the institution—a requirement which we appear to have forgotten in some of our modem edifices, which are colossal structures of brick and cement, but which appear to house very little activity within. In the first place, the seminar and conference rooms had to be acoustically sound and reasonably insulated from activities outside. Secondly, the accommodation and the catering facilities would have to provide the participants with a 'home away from home'. My wife took up the task and entered so zealously into arrangements for furnishing and catering that 'Bella Vista', the place we had taken over for the purpose, was transformed almost overnight. Participants later reported that they felt comfortable and at ease in the atmosphere and surroundings of the college; they did not miss the comforts of a 'home'.

Through, the courtesy of Sir Noel Hall, principal of the Henley Staff College, I was able to obtain valuable advice from the chairman, the Rt. Hon. Heyworth, and members of the Henley College Court of Governors particularly in regard to the method of obtaining qualified staff. In an institution of this kind, not only had the full complement staff to be recruited before the opening of the college, but the staff had to be trained in this particular method of work. At my request, Sir Noel Hall deputed a member of his staff for Hyderabad for a brief period and selected Mr J.W.L. Adame as a member of the directing staff at Henley for the purpose. He had held various important posts before joining the Hyderabad College, and was well qualified was particularly valuable in making the preliminary arrangements in the orientation of the staff and as the first director of studies.

We were privileged to secure the services of Mr Vazifdar of the Textile Group of Tatas, to act as my adviser, and Shri K.T. Chandy one of the directors of Hindustan Lever Ltd, as our first director of research. A little later, Shri A. Zaman, ICS, joined on deputation from the Government of India, Shri Brij Narain, the retired joint secretary of the Union Ministry of Finance and Prof. M.S. Doraiswamy, the retired vice chancellor of the Osmania University joined as full-time members of the faculty. Shri Brij Narain continued in the service of the college for about five years till he was superannuated in 1962, and Prof. Doraiswamy remained at the college for about eight years until he became a member of the Union Public Service Commission in New Delhi. The Government of Andhra Pradesh deputed one of the senior deputy secretaries of the state government, Shri Govindaraja Naidu, to act as the first registrar of the college. Shri V.C. Katoch (later managing director of Indian Detonators Ltd) joined as administrative officer and brought to this task his youth, energy and enthusiasm.

In many scholastic institutions, the participants attend their various courses but take as little as possible interest and in the activities of the institutions during outside hours. Here the principal had to set the 'tone' to induce the participants to want to remain in college outside working hours, engaged in discussion or controversy, in association with their colleagues even though they had got used to a different type of life during their careers.

My wife's arrangements for furnishing and catering made many students feel at home enough to spend time at the college in the evenings. From time to time, a few participants would join us in our rooms in the college, usually over a meal, for friendly discussions about the arrangements, their subjects or the methods for tackling them. Occasionally, I sat with the participants in the evenings to encourage discussions on topics of interest to them and the college.

Again, there was the question of self-discipline, the adherence to strict timings, the necessity to read up the course material for the day, following the decorum of discussion and debate, the bringing out of the experience of each of the participants—all this required a type of self-discipline from the students; and this had to be sedulously encouraged. For example, I noticed one elderly participant, late for his syndicate, trying to gain time by running quickly up the stairs. Later, over a cup of tea, I said to him that doctors advise against running upstairs, but speed did not matter while coming down.

The college soon began to settle down to its normal routine.

Every morning, members are present in their respective syndicate rooms (five in all), after breakfast in the common dining hall. Syndicate leaders take the chair, with the remaining nine members sitting around the syndicate table. Discussions begin punctually at 9 a.m. There are invariably divergent views, as members belong to different organizations in the public and private sectors, as this is usually the first time they are discussing matters outside their own organizations, one sees members of the private sector, as critical of the government and vice versa. But by the end of their three-month stay in the college, they understand one another better. Some members, in defending the views of their organizations, see weaknesses in them by hearing others' views. In this way, they learnt much from each other, and knowledge thus acquired makes a deep impression on their minds.

The working hours of the college, apart from work that is in rooms, are limited to four periods a day—two in the morning, one in the afternoon and one in the late evening.

Each period is ninety minutes in duration. The evenings are devoted to games i.e. tennis, billiards, swimming and miniature golf. There is little time for bridge or other card games, but the lounge contains a variety of newspapers and magazines. There is also a well-equipped library.

The ninety-minute period gives just sufficient time for ten members of the syndicate to make their contribution, provided they are prepared, and the chairman handles the meeting skilfully. A member of the directing staff is in the room, sitting at a separate table from the members of the syndicate. In this way, he is able to watch but not interfere in the discussions as they take place. He usually intervenes when members deviate considerably, or the chairman asks for advice.

The chairman of the syndicate, in conducting discussions, works to a plan and gets an agreed solution to the problem, so that he puts forward the acceptable view of the syndicate at the appointed time to the principal, before all the members of the college and the staff.

The views are presented formally and require an opening speech by each of the five chairmen, explaining the problems, and the chairman's views of how the problem was tackled. The principal sits in front of the five syndicates, on a raised platform and hears the views of each syndicate. He contributes with advice as and when required. At the conclusion of a presentation, the principal gives his comments.

The college has now been running test courses for close to two-and-a-half years, during which time it has been fortunate in receiving, as its early visitors, President Dr Rajendra Prasad, Prime Minister Shri Jawaharlal Nehru, Dr Zakir Hussain, Shri Govind Ballabh Pant, Shri Morarji Desai and several governors of states.

The college was getting accustomed to the syndicate system, and the staff gaining considerable experience in running the syndicates, I was beginning to wonder why Hyderabad College should be wedded to only one system, however good it had turned out to be. The case study method adopted by Harvard had established its reputation throughout the world, and Harvard Business School graduates seemed to be acceptable to all institutions and to be very much in demand. Equally, the Massachusetts Institute of Technology had established a very high reputation for the quality and methods of teaching management and business administration. The California Institute of Technology was also well known for its graduates, both in technology and in administration; while Columbia University had adopted a mixed curriculum, incorporating the different systems then current in the United States. There must be a great deal which 'Hyderabad' could learn from the various 'schools' of administration.

Having examined these systems, I obtained the agreement of the Board of Governors and the government to my detailed study of these systems, somewhat on the lines of my study of the Henley Syndicate system; and was fortunate in the offer of assistance from the Ford Foundation for the purpose of the study. I accordingly obtained my passport, visas and tickets and completed all the various formalities that seemed to beset any departure from these shores. But the journey was not to be.

14

Governor of Assam

One afternoon, my son Satish announced that the home minister was on the phone. I was wondering what had occasioned the call, as I had only spoken to the home minister of Andhra Pradesh that morning. I was taken by surprise when I realized that the call was from Delhi, and a voice said, 'Govind Ballabh Pant speaking.' There was a long enquiry about my family and the health of individual members, but this could not be the reason for a trunk call. I also enquired about Pantji's health. Finally, Pantji asked me how soon I could come to Delhi. As a new session had just started at the college, I suggested some time the following week. 'Yes,' said Pantji, 'Come next week, or tomorrow.'

The next plane reached Delhi in the afternoon, and I found on arrival that Pantji had asked for me to be at his house at 6 p.m. that day, giving me sufficient time to change and reach there. I did not carry any papers with me; as I entered Pantji's room, I felt that the important particulars about the Staff College were well within my memory. The room was a simple one, furnished with the bare necessities, except for an unusual collection of chairs of all shapes and sizes, and a large writing desk covered with books, files and papers. The atmosphere was both business-like and at the same time, calm and serene.

Pantji was sitting at the far end of the writing desk, facing the door, looking a little tired—he had been unwell for some time. He received me warmly, asked me to draw up a chair opposite him, offered me a cup of tea and put me at ease completely with his disarming smile. Just then, his little granddaughter entered the room. Pantji very affectionately told her to come a little later as he was busy with a visitor. His gentleness somehow seemed to generate strength.

My interview started with detailed enquiries about the health of my family; and then Pantji said, 'You know the Governor of Assam Fazal Ali has died. We would like you to go to Assam?' I just managed to suppress the enquiry: 'To do what?' He was obviously telling me that I was required as Governor of Assam, where the North-East Frontier Agency (NEFA) and the Naga Hills were presenting a formidable border and military problems. A Governor with a military background would be of value; and I might be able to assist, though my knowledge of the civilian side was limited. Pantji's next question was characteristic of him: 'How soon can you go?' I said that I would have to consult and obtain the permission of the chairman of the Board of Governors of the college to resign before completing my term. I had also just obtained my passage to the US to see the method of instruction at certain administrative and management educational institutions there, particularly the Harvard case study system. But Pantji, with his characteristic thoroughness and administrative forethought, had, I have no doubt, worked all this out.

When I took his leave, Pantji advised that I had better see the prime minister before returning to Hyderabad. I rang up the PM's secretariat to seek an appointment with him, and I was informed that the PM was away; but, knowing of my arrival, had left a note for me. This the private secretary sent over to Claridges Hotel where I was staying. In this note Pandit Nehru had defined my task as follows:

'You must know, the Governorship of Assam is rather a special one and is in some ways different from that of other normal duties as head of state. In Assam, the Governor is also the agent of the Government of India in regard to NEFA and the Naga Hills and Tuensang Division area. The special assignment is something in addition and involves the personal attention of the Governor. The external affairs ministry deals with these areas; and, as minister of external affairs, I shall be in frequent contact with you.

The Naga Hills and Tuensang area has given us a great deal of trouble, so we have to be vigilant and proceed with caution. Meanwhile, another and serious problem has arisen on our borders with Tibet. The defence of these borders has been put in charge of our Army Headquarters, go far as the NEFA border is concerned, the Governor of Assam will have to pay particular attention to it, naturally in full consultation with the army authorities as well as the Government of India.'

On 14 October 1959, I arrived in Shillong and was sworn in as the Governor of Assam, at a simple ceremony at Raj Bhavan, attended by Chief Minister B.P. Chaliha, members of his cabinet and high officers of the state. Situated on the top of a sloping hill, with the mighty Himalayas in the far distance, a thick surrounding undergrowth and a glistening silvery lake at feet, the picturesque Raj Bhavan in Shillong commands the attention of visitors. The wooden building, though compact and rustic, stands sedate and stately. In its architecture and line, it is a symbol of simple dignity—a home more than an official residence. What contributes much to its character is the fine setting around it—the lovely undulating lawns with majestic pine trees, the riot of exquisite colours, the multitude of flowering shrubs and the profusion of orchids. One cannot imagine a place of such infinite beauty and peace, harbouring an underlying sense of anxiety and charged with trouble in the surrounding areas. Its atmosphere was very soon brought home to me when I entered the porch of Raj Bhavan, and saw the engraving on the wall, facing the entrance, which read, 'My uncle is not greater than my country.' One of the Ahom kings had beheaded his uncle for displaying lack of loyalty to the state.

A couple of days later, I paid a flying visit to NEFA to gain first-hand knowledge of conditions in that area. I had had no experience in direct civil administration; but friends said that it was lucky that I was starting this experience in Assam, where the civil administration, particularly in the tribal areas, might be a little less sophisticated. I could not agree with this view. It seemed to me that the Assamese and the tribal people required an administration carefully trained, highly sensitive and capable of adaptation to the very different social structures of the people of Assam and the hills.

The people of the contiguous hills of NEFA are a lovable race, but it is apparent that they form a somewhat heterogeneous group, with contrasting social backgrounds. They are also very different in themselves from each other. The Monpas in the Kameng Frontier Division are dignified, friendly, hardworking and courteous, with a love for animals and decorative art—to whom ceremonials offer relaxation. The nearby Daflas, on the other hand, are more rustic, with their handicrafts confined to practical requirements; courageous but quarrelsome, living in long family houses with their slaves and servants, but with little conception of village life. Unlike the Monpas, the Daflas, the Mijis (Dhammais) and the Akas are non-Buddhists. The Hill Miris of the Subansari Frontier Division have been described probably too superficially as 'a wild roaming race', artistic but affected by the absence of a well-knit community. The Idu Mishmis are hardy and warlike. Again, there is a contrast between the family social life of the Daflas and Idus, and the life in groups of villages, under a chief, as adopted by the virile Wanchos of the Tirap Frontier Division. The Adis of the Siang Frontier Division, fall into two main groups, the Padams and the Gallongs. The Padam group are distinguished by their cropped hair. Some of the Gallongs still practice polyandry. An important feature of many Adi villages is the dormitory club for boys and men. Some villages also have special clubs for girls. It was evident that these different social and group backgrounds would not permit a stereotyped bureaucratic administration, but would favour a pliant, adaptable form of a coordinating administrative system.

On this first tour of the NEFA, I was struck by the appalling lack of communication. Except for a few airstrips, the approaches to NEFA were limited. It is a hard country; the weather is treacherous, for not only does it rain heavily during the monsoons, but it may also rain at any other time without warning, turning the few roads into quagmires of slippery mud, full of leeches to feed on the passers-by. Hardly any part of NEFA is flat and villages are on steep slopes, where half a million singularly hardy people live in an area of 30,000 sq. miles. There are few outsiders, and the people have not been exploited. They live under special conditions, administer their own custom-based laws and have their own special social set-up. NEFA is, in fact, quite another world, and requires specially trained administrators. The countryside is picturesque, and I was fortunate to get a magnificent bird's-eye view of the snow-clad ranges of the Himalayas, the winding Siang River, the forest-clad hillsides of Mechuka and Tuting, on my first visit to the Divisional Headquarters of the Siang Frontier Division at Along.

In dealings with these people, much depends on how each problem is handled in its initial stage, something on local circumstances and a great deal on the behaviour of local officers at crucial moments. The personal factor is of paramount importance. It is in recognition of this that we have now evolved the pattern of a single-line administration, focused on the political officer in each district. Again, the tendency for administrators, on their first arrival, would be to adopt a paternalistic attitude which comes naturally to most of us—either to treat these tribal areas as museum pieces, or convert them into specimens conforming to our own preconceived notions. Pandit Nehru frequently said, and Shrimati Indira Gandhi has reiterated, that we should allow tribals to develop their own systems of ideas and not permit them to be overwhelmed by the so-called advanced civilization or influenced into becoming a subcaste of the lowest caste of our own Hindu system. So, we have evolved a special technique of administration, with the application of the latest scientific lessons of applied sociology and anthropology. The close contact of our political officers with the people in these areas has also enabled the rapid expansion and consolidation of administration in NEFA, without serious incident, and with peaceful progress, perhaps unparalleled in the history of such areas anywhere in the world. The rapid development of the area and the consolidation of this form of administration have enabled us also to secure, in some measures, our frontiers. A disruption of this consolidation might perhaps have been one of the motives actuating the concentration of the main Chinese attack on this area.

Communication is also a serious problem in this strategic state, which depends for its security on a narrow strip of land near Siliguri in Bengal, as its only land link with India. There is also no all-weather road or rail, linking the eastern districts of Assam, north of the Brahmaputra, with the rest of Assam or with its capital. There were numerous isolated airstrips in this area, (mainly built for the war against Japan in 1941–45), but there was no air link with the capital. An administrative air link, in the form of a small airstrip at Shillong, together with the railway line north of the Brahmaputra, was soon rapidly completed, through the personal interest of the prime minister.

Another problem which engaged attention was what was called the Naga problem. 'Naga' is a general term used to describe some 6 lakh people, living on both sides of the Patkoi range on the Indo–Burmese frontier. Three-and-a-half lakh people live in Nagaland and the remainder in Tirap Frontier Division of NEFA and Manipur. Some Nagas also live on the western borders. Nagas are sturdy and have fine physiques. They are also intelligent and are very shrewd. The usual method of communication amongst themselves is in broken Assamese. There have been periods in history when Naga chiefs even acknowledged the overall sovereignty of the Ahom kings and paid taxes to them in the form of slaves, elephant tusks etc. The early history of British relations with them had been one of constant conflict. The Montagu–Chelmsford Reforms in 1919 described the present Kohima and Mokokchung districts, formerly known as the Naga Hills District, as 'Backward

Tracts' to be 'Excluded Areas', but within the province of Assam. The Governor of Assam remained responsible for administering these areas, acting at his discretion until 15 August 1947. With the inauguration of the Constitution in 1950, the so-called 'administered' area of Tuensang District was incorporated in NEFA and the Governor of Assam administered it at his Discretion, as the agent of the President. The Naga Hills district was administered by the Government of Assam and was subject to the special provisions of the Sixth Schedule of the Constitution of India, which under Article 244 of the Constitution, applies to the administration of the tribal areas of Assam.

It had gradually become evident that the Nagas would not be satisfied with this kind of set-up and wanted the areas inhabited by them to be grouped as a single administrative unit, under some form of regional autonomy; and demands to this effect had been voiced before Sir Akbar Hydari, the then Governor of Assam. The vehicle for the expression of these demands was the Naga National Council, originally a government body constituted in 1945–46 to improve the political and economic conditions of the Nagas through constitutional means. While the Naga National Council did not, within the first instance, concern itself much in political activity, it came gradually under the influence of the Naga leader,

Zapu Phizo, who held strong views in favour of the complete independence of the Naga people.

Sir Akbar Hydari, held prolonged talks with Phizo and the Naga National Council, as a result of which, a nine-point memorandum known as the Hydari Agreement was drawn up in 1947, providing for the administration of the Nagas as part of Assam, but under the aegis of the Governor. According to Clause 9 of this agreement, at the end of ten years from the day it came into effect, 'the Nagas were to be given the choice of an extension of the Agreement'. The intention, of course, was that at the end of this period of ten years, the Nagas would be free to suggest, if they so wished, an administrative pattern to suit their special genius and to ensure a more developed system of autonomy within India. Extremist Nagas, however, misinterpreted this article to mean that the Nagas had the option to demand complete independence.

Our policy has always been to give the fullest autonomy and opportunity of self-development to the Naga people, without interfering in any way in their internal affairs or their way of life. Unfortunately, the process of evolution of local autonomy could not be implemented in full, because troubles arose in the area as a result of the hostile activities of the section of the Nagas under Phizo's leadership, ostensibly to carve out an independent Naga territory entirely separate from India. This was a demand which no government could concede.

The hostile elements among the Naga people, thereupon took to violent methods. The cooperation of the people in general was lacking and the role given to the army was to take action against the Naga hostiles, at the same time preventing hardship to innocent people. This made the conduct of military operations difficult, and consequently, the conflict continued for a long time. The hostile Nagas, however, did not hesitate to cause suffering to those who were not actively with them, many of whom were anxious to live a peaceful life and carry on their own avocations.

It had now become apparent that there were elements amongst the Nagas, who were repelled by Phizo's policy of extreme violence. There were also growing indications of a split in the Naga National Council, within which was emerging a moderate section, who felt that Phizo's methods of extreme violence were not in the ultimate interest of the Nagas themselves and that it would be better to proceed along more peaceful and constitutional lines.

Phizo, however, was determined by every means, including violence and murder, to put a stop to these modern elements, which were growing in strength, and he even manipulated the killing of his own secretary, Shri Sakhrie, whom he suspected of being opposed to his policy of independence. Sakhrie was a brilliant, widely respected young man, and his murder had the effect of opening the eyes of the people to Phizo's violent fanaticism. Phizo found it necessary, eventually, to leave the Naga Hills and cross over to Burma, giving over local charge of the independence movement to the vice president of the Naga National Council, Imkongmeren Ao. Perhaps he also felt that by going abroad, he could canvass the support of other nations and the UN in his demand for Naga sovereignty.

A strong section of the Naga population recognized that the demand for separation from India was unrealistic and that a campaign of violence was futile. The liberal leaders, at great personal risk, also began to assert themselves and openly condemned the hostile movement. In the summer of 1957, the Nagas convened an All-Tribes Naga People's Convention in Kohima. It was attended by 1765 delegates and over 2000 visitors representing every tribe and area of the territory then forming part of the Naga Hills District of Assam and the Tuensang Frontier Division of NEFA. This came to be known as the First Convention; it passed a number of resolutions, one of which, on 1 December 1957, led to the creation of a single administrative unit, the Naga Hills Tuensang Area (NHTA) under the Ministry of External Affairs, to be administered by the Governor as the agent of the President of India. The Naga people hoped that the formation of a new unit would give them an opportunity of developing their area, in the way they considered best suited to their needs. Some progress was no doubt made, but the activities of the hostile elements stood in the way of normal development.

A second Naga People's Convention was held in Ungma, a large village near Mokokchung, in May 1958. It was this convention which ultimately led to the birth of the new state of Nagaland within the Indian Union. It also appointed a Liaison Committee to contact the underground elements and get their support to the policy of securing the maximum autonomy for their area. Though some among the hostile elements appreciated this approach, their response was generally not encouraging. The Naga people, therefore, decided to get on with their plan for a final political settlement without the help of the hostiles, and called a Third Convention at Mokokchung in October 1959. Again, the main demand formulated by the Nagas at this convention was for the constitution of a separate state within the Indian Union to be known as Nagaland, under the Ministry of External Affairs, with a government, a secretariat, a council of ministers and a Legislative Assembly.

In July 1960, the prime minister received a delegation of fifteen Naga leaders led by Dr Imkongliba Ao, president of the Naga People's Convention and a broad agreement was reached. The overriding necessity was to win every influential Naga, whatever their background, into as friendly a frame of mind as was possible, so that the state could ultimately settle down with its people, and the people accept, without any mental reservation, the citizenship of India.

With the introduction of political reforms, the setting up of an interim body and the functioning of executive councillors as de facto ministers, in terms of the Delhi Agreement, the political situation in Nagaland entered a new phase, and the people began showing unusual vitality in reconstructing their disturbed economy. But though there was considerable change, the problem was far from solved, as there were still several areas where conditions remained unsettled. So, military pressure continued, and the underground rebels were relentlessly chased. At the same time, the regrouping of villages served to deprive the underground Nagas of much of their local support. Further, the inauguration of the Nagaland state, on 1 December 1963, with the autonomy it granted, enabled the Naga intelligentsia to appreciate the benefits conferred by the new reforms.

This was the moment chosen by New Delhi to make conciliatory gestures to the underground Nagas and to invite the Peace Mission, initiated by the Church Leaders to 'open the dialogue' between government and the Naga underground (movement). Unfortunately, this move gave the Naga underground (movement) the much-needed respite, while waiting for fresh reinforcements to be trained outside India. They took full advantage of the lull brought about by the proposed negotiations, through delayed replies and desultory talks.

At last, on 13 August, an agreement was reached for the suspension of operations with reciprocal obligations by the hostiles. However, the reciprocal obligations were disregarded, and the Naga hostiles established themselves as a parallel government, by sending armed men into villages, collecting fines and punishing loyal Nagas. They also continued to snipe at and ambush the security forces.

The first peace talks took place on 22 September and the negotiations dragged on interminably. Indian forces looked on impotently while the agreement for suspension of hostilities continued to be flouted, while demands were successively raised and equally successively conceded in part or whole.

On one occasion, the hostiles even objected at the conference to the presence of Shilu Ao, the chief minister of Nagaland, though the agreement had accepted representation for the Nagaland government. This demand was virtually conceded by naming Shila Ao as a member of the Indian Central delegation. The hostiles, designing themselves as the Nagaland Federal Government, now claimed to negotiate on equal terms. This the Government of India attempted to counter by a declaration that they did not recognize that right. Later, the hostiles demanded that the Government of India delegation be raised to a ministerial level. This demand was further escalated for talks at the summit between the two prime ministers. The meetings with Prime Minister Nehru were held, though it was stated that such a demand would net be agreed to unless the principle of settlement within the Indian Constitution was accepted. To make matters worse, the hostiles were permitted to celebrate Republic Day at the headquarters of the local government, with the President's speech hurling defiance at the Government of India. I cannot believe that the Nagas alone were behind all this. They have been greatly encouraged by China and Pakistan, but equally so has been the support given to them by the leaders of various foreign religious missions residing in Nagaland.

It had been the Government of India's stand that no agreement could be reached except within the framework of the Indian Constitution. So at least, in that context, it was necessary at some stage of the negotiations, to declare emphatically that talks could not continue, except on the clear acceptance of this principle. But this does not appear to have been done.

On the other hand, during this whole period, concessions continued to be granted, starting from the Hydari Agreement recognizing the rights of the Nagas to develop within

India, according to their own desires; continuing through the acceptance in 1957 of the demand that Nagaland and Tuensang Division be treated as a separate unit, and later placed directly under the central government and finally through an agreement to treat this amalgamated Nagaland as a full-fledged state. Now at least the plan of the Peace Mission, stated below, might have been made the basis for further discussion. But, although the plan had been accepted by the Government of India, it had not yet elicited a firm response from the Naga underground (movement), because of the belief perhaps, that further concessions will be forthcoming as the 'dialogue' continued.

The Peace Mission's main recommendation was on the one hand, Nagaland could, on their own volition, decide to be a participant in the Union of India and mutually settle the terms and conditions for the purpose. On the other hand, the Government of India could consider to what extent the pattern and structure of the relationship between Nagaland and the Government of India should be adopted and recast as to satisfy the political aspirations of all sections of Naga opinion.

In the present atmosphere, while no formula implying secession can be acceptable to any government, the Government of India stands committed to the grant of the fullest possible, internal autonomy, providing the

Naga extremists with a face-saving device. If, at the end of a reasonable stipulated period, the Nagaland Federal Government leaders fail to respond favourably, the Government of India appears to have no alternative but to renew action against the armed rebellion, but on this occasion giving the security forces full authority to deal with the situation more militarily. We naturally have to show patience in the hope that we will not have to reverse our present generous policy, but we have seen that patience is sometimes apt to be mistaken for weakness. On the other side, the Naga extremists have been saying, 'Nagaland has always been an independent territory, adjoining the territories of Assam and Burma. If India is not prepared to concede sovereign Independence, would India prefer to exterminate the Nagas?' The statement of the problem in this form shows how much it is charged with emotion.

Undoubtedly, the Naga problem is a special one and no single line of approach will see its solution. Fortunately, we now have many more Nagas looking for peaceful development as a part of India than we had four years ago.

Recently, Nagaland has been formally inaugurated as the sixteenth state of India, with its own capital at Kohima and a Governor and a high court common with Assam. The prime minister, Shrimati Indira Gandhi, had herself received in Delhi delegations representing the hostiles.

She carried with her the good wishes of the entire country, in finding a solution to a conflict that has resulted, for so many years, in so much needless distress and loss of life. At the same time, it appears to me that, on our part, we must continue relentlessly our military pressure against those who believe in violence, for the Nagas also respect firm handling.

For an administrator, Assam is an interesting state. Geographically, it has a character that is unique, because of its extraordinary diversity. A visitor can pass in a day from the humid flat waterlogged lands of the Cachar–Gauhati [sic] areas, scattered with abrupt little hills, to the undulating grassy scenery of upper Assam. He can divert his course to the rolling downs of the Khasi hills, or to the beautiful mixed scenery of the NEFA, Mizo and Naga hills; or even venture into the magnificent awe-inspiring grandeur of the Himalayas. A visitor can also enjoy his fishing or golf in numerous beautiful spots of the state or visit the well-known game Sanctuary of Kaziranga—the home of the one-horned rhinoceros. But, in the Naga Hills and NEFA area, the visitor will be surprised by the paucity of birds.

To an administrator, however, the geographical borders of Tibet, Burma and East Pakistan also lend colour to the problems with which he deals. These problems are enhanced by the ethnic pockets formed by isolation in hill tracts or thick jungles. The area itself is a meeting place for three races, the Polynesian, the Aryan and the Mongolian. Ethnologically, it gives a varied and interesting background. The Buddhist religion was born not far from Assam, and the Hindu religion has given the state its basic philosophy, but quite a few areas are under Christian and Muslim influence. All this has been superimposed on a native humanistic philosophy, suited to the isolated pockets in which large parts of the population live. Historically and politically, this has been a turbulent area, the plains people being more lethargic in temperament, but more subject to the changing influences of modern culture.

It is no wonder then, that Assam is a problem state, with many centrifugal forces. To these, we have added the question of language. The more educated migrant from over-populated Bengal often captures the trade and the business opportunities of the tract and the local resident sometimes feels he is being exploited. Similarly, the hill people tend to be suspicious of the plainsmen; and, largely because of the social changes that are taking place, the plainsmen treat the hillmen as 'tribals'. These inter-communal rivalries are enhanced by very poor communications and the absence of a uniform level of education. Such isolation accentuates the desire of each community to have a greater and greater share in its own destiny and reduces the appreciation of the value of a joint unified approach. The ever-riding problem of Assam, therefore, is one of integration, with the improvement of physical communication, with the encouragement of inter-racial exchange, and with an appreciation of the advantages of federated effort on a statewide scale.

As if these problems in themselves were not of sufficiently large dimensions, nature appears also to have conspired to contribute. For example, there are high-intensity earthquakes, which have prevented buildings of normal heavy construction—yet when tremors come, the specially constructed wooden buildings also collapse and render people homeless. Raj Bhavan collapsed in the earthquake in the 1890s but stood mainly intact after the 1950 quake. Such lightly constructed wooden buildings increase dangers of fires, generally through the disruption of the electric system. The popular Shillong Club—which is a good meeting place for people from all the mofussil areas—was only a few years ago burnt to the ground within a few minutes. At the same time, Assam registers the highest rainfall in the world, over 600 inches per annum, all in the short rainy season, at Cherrapunji, close to Shillong, in the Khasi Hills.

Each year, the mighty Brahmaputra goes into spate and destroys lives and property, carries away people, cattle and land, and inundates vast areas. In the Mizo hills, a famine called by the Mizo's 'Mautam', occurs periodically as a result of the growth in the population of rats. Apparently, this takes place at the time of the flowering of the bamboo, and according to general belief, once in every fifty years, when people die by the thousands. Fortunately, this fiftieth-year scourge, on this occasion, gave us a warning; for example, when rats devoured the October paddy harvest. Essential commodities like food grains, sugar, salt etc., were airlifted at subsidized rates because cash crops are not easily marketable on account of difficult communications; and all possible measures were taken against famine and also against the rats. It is understandable, therefore, that the people of Assam, who have to face such momentous onslaughts of nature are noted for their fortitude and are zealous of their individuality.

To a normal man, a setback in health is generally unpalatable. To me, who had prided myself on my physical fitness and proficiency in sports, a tremor which developed in my left leg was difficult to accept. So, after consulting Maj. (now Lt Col) K.L. Chopra of the Shillong Military Hospital and Col Inder Singh, medical adviser to the army, I underwent an operation in the UK which was advised by Dr Dennis Williams, physician at the National Hospital and performed by Mr Lawrence Walsh at the Atkinson Morley Hospital, Wimbledon, where I had been admitted.

On my visit to London for this purpose, Mrs Vijaya Lashmi Pandit very kindly invited us to stay and made very comprehensive arrangements, which, in view of the tremor

I had developed, were very welcome. But I was somewhat embarrassed by my not being able to see my hostess, as she was extremely busy—a natural situation in view of her position as high commissioner in the UK. I was further embarrassed when Mrs Pandit asked me to see her and seemed a little upset at the daily telephonic enquiries from Panditji about the operation. She made detailed enquiries about the doctors and the nature of the operation, and she took personal interest in the arrangements for the operation.

Mr Lawrence Walsh is a lightly built man, barely five feet in height, yet he surprised me by being fully up during the four-hour strenuous ordeal of the operation. I was fortunate in that the operation was completely successful, and I returned to India within a month, fit and well. Unfortunately, a year later, when I was in Hyderabad, another tremor started in the other leg. So, I took another month's leave and went to the same doctor for an operation on the other side. Specialists in London pronounced me cured and fit to resume my duties. One of them told my wife, in a typical British manner, 'Your husband's heart ticks better than mine, even though I am ten years younger.' The second operation, however, was not as successful as the first, and I have had to resort to regular medication since.

15

Governor of Andhra Pradesh

In July 1962, Prime Minister Pandit Jawaharlal Nehru invited me to take over the governorship of the state of Andhra Pradesh. I was sorry to leave Assam, as I was attached to its people and had become conversant with their problems. Andhra Pradesh was a different type of responsibility—that of a purely constitutional Governor of one of our larger states, and it would afford a fresh experience. Besides, Hyderabad was my hometown, and I had happy recollections of my stay in that city. So, early in September 1962, I bade farewell to Assam, and after a few days' halt in Delhi arrived in Hyderabad on the 7 September.

By coming to Hyderabad, I had returned to the place of my early childhood. It was almost thirty years since my father had passed away in Hyderabad. As he was a pioneer in anaesthesia and bacteriology, and as he had also done some original work on plague (his research was published in Germany), he had been much in demand as a physician. I well remember the number of carriages and cars that lined the drive leading to our house every evening, awaiting his return from the office. In this period, he made a number of friends. It was with deep emotion, that after this long lapse of time, I received several letters of good wishes from my father's friends on my appointment to Andhra Pradesh. My father's life was devoted to his work; and I was happy that I, too, was now allowed to serve in the place where he had lived and worked.

It was Hyderabad that, at the age of nineteen, I first put on a military uniform, upon receiving my commission in the army, and it was at Hyderabad, at the Fateh Maidan, that I attended my last parade as Chief of the Army Staff. It was to Hyderabad again that I came after my retirement, to establish the Administrative Staff College. Hyderabad had, therefore, associations connected with some of the most significant events in my life.

Andhra Pradesh is a state with several special features. It is linguistically carved out, largely from the Deccan plateau, comprising what was once the princely state of Hyderabad and the Telugu-speaking area of the former bilingual state of Madras. It contains large forests and dry scrubby areas with unusual rock formations. In some parts rice is grown in abundance, which would be supplemented in no small measure by the development of the Nagarjunasagar Multipurpose Dam and Pochampadu irrigation projects. Nagarjunasagar is a splendid example of a labour-intensive project, a type which is economically of great value to India, because of the small proportion of foreign exchange involved in comparison to the local resources employed. The state has a coastline of some 600 miles, on which lies Waltair, one of the most beautiful seaside towns in India. Waltair (Vishakhapatnam) is a prosperous town of importance and the seat of Andhra University.

Andhra Pradesh's population of 38 million, largely rural, is predominantly, Hindu; but the ruling class of the former Hyderabad state had been Muslim for over three centuries, a fact which left a visible mark on its culture. Partly, this was due to the style of living of the upper classes, especially the nobility, who lived in large comfortable places with extensive grounds surrounded by high walls (a characteristic of Hyderabad) and especially the upper middle classes. They all kept a sumptuous table, a big retinue of servants and dependants and lived in style. My father had many friends among them. Early in my life, I had met many of the noblemen and was impressed by their courtesy and good manners. Many 'Mulkis' will remember Nawab Sir Salar Jung, Raja Rai, Nawab Lutf-ud-Dowlah Bahadur, Nawab Wali-ud-bowlah Bahadur, Nawab Fareed Nawaz Jung Bahadur, Nawab Bashir-ud-Dowlah Bahadur, Maharaja Kishan Pershad, Raja Rumbha Rao and other similar dignitaries.

The state's last Muslim ruler, His Exalted Highness, the late Nizam of Hyderabad, a direct descendant of one of Emperor Aurangzeb's generals, met me at Raj Bhavan soon after I assumed office. He appeared remarkably alert, considering that he was over eighty years of age at the time. The last time I had met him was at his residence at King Kothi Palace, to call on him with my father. The Nizam was very gracious and made detailed enquiries about my mother and other members of our family, though nearly thirty years had elapsed since our first meeting.

The capital town of Andhra Pradesh, Hyderabad, once the Nizam's capital, presents an attractive mixture of the old and the new and used to be a centre of Muslim culture and learning. The state has two official languages, Telugu and Urdu. About five miles west of the city is the massive Golconda Fort and the tomb of the Qutab Shahi Kings, who ruled the Deccan during the sixteenth and seventeenth centuries. Golconda Fort is so well-sited and constructed that it has never been captured in battle, except once by Aurangzeb, and that only after ten years of siege and its betrayal by a traitor in the service of the Golconda ruler.

The presence of the British cantonments at Bolarum, Trimulgherry and Secunderabad is a testimony to the respect that the British had for the fighting man of south India.

After Independence, the state passed through a difficult period. The British were quitting India and all princely states had to choose accession to either one or the other dominion.

Britain's view was that the princes of India had freedom of choice.

But it had not given sufficient weight to the fact that Pakistan was formed out of the conception of a purely religious (Muslim) state, while India proposed to remain secular. The problem was further complicated because of geographical and other considerations.

The Nizam's territory was completely surrounded by the Indian Union. The majority of the Hyderabadi population was Hindu; the ruler was Muslim. What would be Hyderabad's position? The late Nizam felt that Hyderabad should remain independent and not accede to either dominion. This was a position that neither dominion could accept, more particularly India which completely encircled it.

The situation worsened with the advent of new political parties which came on the scene within the state. The Ittehadul Muslimeen, an extremist Muslim organization, with its militant wing, the Razakars, became active and demanded accession to Pakistan.

The law and order situation got out of control on the creation of aggressive irregular forces by the Razakars, and the Indian government was forced to intervene.

Southern Command, under the leadership of the late Lt Gen. Rajendra Singhji was asked to prepare a plan for a police action against Hyderabad. The force used was to consist largely of armoured units and was placed under the command of Maj. Gen. (later Gen.) J.N. Chaudhuri. The day was 13 September 1948. The armour used by the Indian force outstripped Hyderabad's forces in quantity and quality, and there was hardly any resistance. In five days, the operation was over.

This historic state also contains one of India's most sacred place of pilgrimage, Tirupati, the abode of the Lord of the Seven Hills and the home of one of the richest temples in southern India. The temple is a fine example of early Dravidian art. Again, the state contains the shrine of Srisailam, another important pilgrimage centre for worshippers of Shiva.

I was impressed by the former administration of Hyderabad. It had built up efficient water supply systems in the Husainsagar and Nizamsagar lakes. It had cement roads traversing the major parts of the city and forming important trans-state highways. It had also an imposing high court, an extensive and modern hospital and the Osmania University, where a high standard was set in the regional language (Urdu). A major part of this improvement had been undertaken during the regime of the present Nizam.

The rural areas, however, had not received the same high level of attention.

A place of much interest, having old associations for me, was the Salar Jung Museum. This was probably the greatest one-man collection in the world, of curiosities of every conceivable kind. Nawab Salar Jung, a former prime minister of the Hyderabad state and the owner of the museum, kept neither lists nor records of the articles he acquired, either of old manuscripts or of valuable pieces of jewellery or ancient weapons. Yet he knew where every article was kept. When he entered a shop, he rarely made single purchases, but took all that there was on the shelf.

I had a standing invitation to his palace, when I was stationed there as a young Subaltern. The Nawab sahib was a bachelor, charming and hospitable. On his death in 1949, his residence in the city was taken over by the Government of India because of its historic contents, to be used as a National Museum; and a board was appointed with the Governor as its chairman to look after and preserve its treasures. As the chairman of the board, I found that some of the contents of the building were not worth the effort required for storing. So, suitable staff were appointed to sort out the valuables and list them in a catalogue. As the existing building had become very dilapidated, it was decided to construct a new building on the site donated by the Salar Jung Estate, on the bank of the River Musa, for its further development into a modern national museum.

The Andhra Pradesh government was stable, and the general economic and political situation in the state was satisfactory. The financial position, however, was not so sound, because of expenditure on numerous development projects in the state, some of which when completed, would benefit other parts of India, as well as the state itself. I, therefore, supported the state government's view that the centre should take over the Nagarjunasagar and Pochampadu irrigation projects and the proposed electricity project at Srisailam.

On 20 October 1962, that is, only a month or so after I arrived at Hyderabad, the Chinese attacked our frontier in NEFA, clearing India's forces from some 35,000 sq. miles of frontier. A physical map of China would show the low-lying fertile regions.

These are studded with mountains, plains along its west coast. But nowhere are they much higher than 5000 ft. This area has a rainfall of approximately forty inches and is irrigated by the lower reaches of the Yellow and the Yangtze rivers. An approximate line drawn from Peking to Hanoi would roughly mark the western limit of this 'rice-bowl' of China, the home of the Han race. Chinese culture, wealth, industry and almost 80 per cent of her population are concentrated in this eastern region. Further west, the mountains rise from 5000 to 8000 ft, and the rainfall decreases from forty inches to ten inches. The rivers flow through deep gorges, and irrigation is not possible except in the river valleys. Here millet and wheat are grown.

The rest of China, which comprises almost half the land mass, rises to heights above the tree line. The Gobi desert in the north and the high Tibetan plateau in the west, make it difficult to inhabit these areas, except along the river valleys.

This geographical division has influenced the people who inhabited these regions and moulded their history. The people of the rich rice bowl tended to be ease-loving. The people of the millet–wheat belt were hardier; and whenever the crops failed, they raided the rich plains of the east. The nonds, inhabiting the western region, were even more war-like and depended mainly on their animals. From time immemorial, natural calamities, or the lure of plunder, made them invade and ransack the wealth of the plainsmen.

It is from these regions that some of the great Mongol conquerors, like Genghis Khan, carved out empires and overran Central Asia.

These constant raids into the plains led to the concept and construction of the Great Wall of China. The security afforded by it, and the resources of the area contributed to the rise and growth of the ancient kingdoms of China. With greater wealth and power, the rulers of China gradually started expanding northwards, subduing the nomadic tribes. This process went on for some 2000–3000 years, the pressure increasing or decreasing with the power and decay of the empire, until Manchuria, Mongolia, Sinkiang, Tibet, Yuman and Annam were subdued and made part of China. With such a historical background of the last 3000–4000 years, it would not be wrong to assume that the Chinese have always been expansionist throughout their long history.

The estimated cultivable land in India is 322 million acres, while that in China is in the region of 3000 million acres. Chinese population approximately one-and-a-half times that of India, is growing at an estimated rate of 30 million annually, and may touch a thousand million mark in the eighties of this century. While, however, China's population will undoubtedly grow, her cultivable land cannot increase.

But China's agricultural practices are better than those of India. It is already producing two crops annually in the rice bowl, though this does not leave sufficient margin to meet the demands of the exploding population. There is little doubt, therefore, that it will have to seek food farther afield.

There are only two regions in the world which are surplus in food—North America and southeast Asia. The latter consists of small, unstable, weak countries, rich not only in surplus food but other strategic commodities such as rubber, tin, minerals and oil. The conclusion appears to be that China's long-term aim must be to control or subjugate, in due course, the whole of Southeast Asia. This would threaten the security of India from the north and east and through the southern seas unless the continued independence of those smaller countries is assured.

Not only is China historically and economically expansionist but ideologically too it follows the communist theory of expansionism and believes in overthrowing (other) states by force. There was but one communist state in the early twenties, with 100 million people converted to the 'faith' through force. Today, that is in just four decades, a third of the world, with a thousand million people, live under communism. No faith in the world has exploded so rapidly to such great dimensions. While Russia had developed considerably through the implementation of her several plans in the last four decades and has a great deal to lose in the event of war, China continues to believe in militant force. Their leaders have made unequivocal statements on the subject. In the last thirteen years of her existence, China has resorted to the use of force in

Korea, Indo–China (mainland southeast Asia), Sinkiang, Tibet and India. Once again, the conclusion appears to be that China is, historically, economically and ideologically expansionist.

What is China's potential for expansion? The size of her armed forces and militia run into millions, and the fact that it has the third-largest air force in the world is well known. What is perhaps less known is that her industrial potential is growing at a rate faster than that of India. Like all communist states, it is concentrating on the rapid growth of these industries that make the state militarily strong.

The international boundary between India and China has this special feature. On the Indian side, it slopes southward to the fertile plains; on the Chinese side, it enters a nearly barren plateau interspersed with very high ranges and little population. India would gain nothing by crossing this boundary, while China could dominate the fertile plains in the south. India is, thus, more sensitive to any conflict, than China could ever be.

Against this background, we find China surreptitiously intruding into Indian territory by building the Aksai Chin Road in Ladakh in 1957. In NEFA, our borders appeared more secure, especially as the Chinese Prime Minister Zhou Enlai, during his visit to India in 1956, pointedly informed his Indian counterpart that his government had accepted the formalization of the McMahon Line in the case of Burma and proposed to recognize it in the case of India. Despite this assurance, China began in 1962 to 'creep forward' south of Tibet, and by so doing created a threat across the traditional Indo–China border in NEFA also. As we could not accept this risk, our government ordered its troops in NEFA to take up positions closer to the border, but well within our own territory. This was a political decision arising out of growing Indian public pressure which demanded some action to meet the Chinese threat. China appears to have interpreted this move as likely to frustrate her plans, and it crossed the NEFA boundary in the region of Thagla on 8 September 1962, apparently to prevent consolidation of our defences in this area. We naturally resisted and called for discussions to settle matters peacefully.

China then broke all pretence of friendly relations and launched an attack against India on both the eastern and western sections of NEFA. Just as suddenly, on 21 November 1962, China announced a unilateral ceasefire and the withdrawal of her troops behind positions held by her in October 1959. It was hoped that this would gain world sympathy, by pretending to establish peaceful intentions for the settlement of the border issue, whilst at the same time holding on to the Aksai Chin area occupied

in the first 'creep forward' as well as the area near Thagla
ridge, which it occupied in September 1962.

On the other hand, would it not be more correct to
say that the Chinese forces in NEFA had overstretched
themselves, and got themselves enmeshed in the
Himalayas? At about that time, the passes were closing,
and communications were becoming almost impossible.
The result was that a large Chinese force was collected on
the southern side and would be cut off as soon as the passes
stopped functioning without adequate logistic support,
and these troops could have been annihilated by us if we
had built up any reserve force to support our troops in
the forward line. It appears that the ceasefire was perhaps
a convenient way for the Chinese to extricate themselves
from their positions in NEFA. It would appear also that
even if adequate troops had been withdrawn by us in time
from other fronts to fight in NEFA, they would not have
been trained for such fighting, nor indeed did they have
the right clothing and equipment for such an undertaking.

All of us experienced a deep sense of mortification
and shame when the ineffectiveness of the strategy we
had adopted became apparent, soon after the Chinese
launched their main assault. All the teaching of military
strategy, which had been inculcated in us from the start
of our careers! The nature of that terrain gave the Chinese

easier lines of communication at the higher altitude and gave us the most difficult ones. The knowledge about our unpreparedness for a war in that area and at those heights, dictated that we should have met the assault by opposition at those places where our lines of communications were shortest and easiest, and the enemies extenuated and more difficult. All these factors dictated that we should have challenged the enemy at lower altitudes and not so far forward. This would have meant, of course, the temporary vacation of much ground. But opposing them at lower altitudes would have given us further time to make certain that the passes were closed behind the Chinese forces.

But a different strategy seems to have been adopted at the last moment, and at too late a stage for even our troops to be suitably equipped or logistically supplied. Everyone knows that plainsmen going for the first time to a height of 10,000 ft find breathing difficult and every step becomes an effort, because of lack of oxygen. Yet this changed strategy required men to be taken from the plains to altitudes over 14,000 ft and expected of them not only to be active there but to fight with vigour, without proper clothing or equipment.

What deepened the sense of mortification and shame was that the debacle had occurred to some of our better units (Fourth Division), which had shown their hardihood, courage and fighting qualities in the Second World War. The debacle also shattered their morale, a tragedy of which Pakistan was to try and take advantage of three years later. Whilst China acted thus, the Colombo Powers—the six non-aligned Afro–Asian powers—met and put forward proposals to get India and China to the conference table. Briefly, these proposals were for China to retreat twenty kilometres in Ladakh from the positions it had gained, and India not to move forward from the positions it had been forced back to. The area between the two lines was to be treated as a demilitarized zone, administered through civil posts from both sides in NEFA and China was to withdraw north of the McMahon Line except at the two passes. India also moved its administration up to the McMahon Line.

We accepted the Colombo proposals. But China wanted India to concede her claim to Aksai Chin in exchange for her recognition of a boundary north of Assam, which would approximate to the McMahon Line. How could India accept the transfer of a vast part of her territory taken by aggression, especially when there was no guarantee that similar losses would not occur in future? So, there was no progress towards a mutually acceptable settlement.

Much has been written about the lessons taught us by the Chinese aggression. I cannot help feeling that many of such lessons would have been automatically apparent had we adopted the top defence organizational structure mentioned in an earlier chapter. For, in this crisis, the government had no full-time organization to give them a combined defence view of the sudden and tense situation which faced us at that time.

I toured the state of Andhra Pradesh to raise the general consciousness of our people to the danger from China. I found that the Chinese attack had shaken the country, but the nation was facing this challenge magnificently. Our petty controversies stopped overnight, and there was remarkable unity throughout the country.

The saying that 'nothing succeeds like success' points also to the complimentary adage that morale is one of the essentials of success. Had Pakistan attacked us two years earlier or even one year earlier, their assault could not, I fear, have been so easily blunted. It takes time for morale to be rebuilt, particularly in the older officers and men, and by the time Pakistan attacked us in 1965, our shattered morale had not yet been completely restored. Pakistan attempted to delay that restoration by propaganda—that Indians would not 'fight'. However, such propaganda did not delay the build-up of our morale. On the contrary, it might even have led to the opposite result.

However, our wars appear to have emphasized certain primary principles that all nations appear to forget at one time or another. Once we are involved in war, military strategy must dictate clearly the objectives, which are based on the aim of destroying the enemy's forces and making ineffective their vital centres of communications, and these objectives must be ruthlessly achieved.

The same principles appear to be applicable to the involvement of the USA in Indo–China. They must either get out of their involvement or ensure that the objectives are achieved ruthlessly and irrespective of other considerations if they are not to suffer ignominious defeat. These principles have been learnt by us in our own generation; as lessons from our own involvements. Let us hope that this and the succeeding generations do not forget them.

16

Governor of Mysore

At the Governor's Conference in November 1965, it was suggested to me that adjustments in certain political appointments in the country would necessitate my transfer to Mysore, and I accordingly moved to that state early in the following year.

In Mysore, there had been since Independence a Governor well suited to the state—the maharaja—who was the ruler before India achieved freedom. He was deeply religious, respected and loved by his people for his progressive policies.

The Government of India, however, felt it necessary to make a change and to introduce in that state its system of constitutional governors. This became a problem, as the public feeling had, by that time, veered around in favour of traditional heads of state like the maharajas. As a nation, we are fond of pageantry and are loyal to tradition. In many places, the previous ruling princes were being elected as people's representatives, in preference to other political leaders.

To take the place of the Maharaja of Mysore, whose family had been traditional rulers of this state for generations, was a delicate and difficult assignment.

The replacement would have to be a non-controversial figure. He would have to be correct in all his public utterances, both from the point of view of the government as well as the public; and by his conduct, he would gradually have to obtain the acceptance of the public.

This assignment was also not without personal embarrassment for me. The language of the state was Kannada, with which I was not familiar. In Mysore, as in other southern states, the agitation against Hindi had aroused the people, and the importance of the state language was being emphasized. It would be difficult for me to speak in Kannada until I had been long enough in Mysore to pick up that language. It was becoming increasingly clear that very soon an Indian would be looked upon as a stranger in any state other than his own unless he knew the local language.

The Maharaja of Mysore, first as a ruler and later as the Governor, had been using his palaces in Mysore and Bangalore for his residential and official purposes. Consequently, when I came to Bangalore on 4 May 1964, I found there was no official residence for the Governor. Chief Minister Shri Nijalingappa hoped that the Governor would reside in Bangalore, the capital of Mysore state, rather than in Mysore, where the Maharaja had his main palace; and, on my arrival, allotted to me one of the State

Guest House in Bangalore, known as the Residency. This was later converted, at my suggestion, into the Raj Bhavan for Mysore state.

Fortunately, the 'breaking-in' period of the change, from the traditional and revered head of the state to that of a constitutional governor, passed off smoothly.

Because of my previous experience in two states, first Assam, in which a greater part of my time had been spent on directly administering the special areas, and in Andhra Pradesh, where (as in Mysore) the Governor had no direct responsibility for administration of his own, but was a representative of the President, and the link between the Centre and the states, I spent quite a little time ruminating on the exact role and tasks of this office.

To a soldier, the task appeared more than a little complicated and a trifle confused. Whenever India was under one rule, it had always adopted a unitary system of governance with a strong Centre, whether under Chandragupta, under the Moguls [sic] or under the British. On the other hand, we had now embarked on a federal system, without all the characteristics of a true federation, and with special peculiarities of its own. The system we had adopted seemed suited for the encouragement of separatist movements, but for the unifying factors of the supremacy of the Constitution and the difficulty of any change in it, and the power of the Constitution to interpret the validity or invalidity of Acts passed by the Legislature or actions performed by the Executive. A third unifying factor was the fact that the Centre and the states were largely controlled by one party, but this was not a permanent situation and would not necessarily continue.

Recently, the former two factors have become prominent by events in West Bengal where recognizable offences were committed by organized groups against management personnel and executives of the government, and the police were forbidden from taking action, in contravention of precepts of the Indian Penal Code. The high court's assistance was found necessary to ensure that the police took action, as enjoined by law, of recognizable offences. Again, in West Bengal, the High Court's support had been sought and obtained to uphold the writ of the Governor, when he considered it necessary to dismiss the ministry, which he felt no longer commanded a majority in the assembly.

There are also indirect factors which help to keep together the federal units, the most important of which is of course the allocation of financial resources, particularly when most of the states are unable to meet their expenses and have to depend financially on the Centre; and also, the removal of such subjects like defence and external affairs from the jurisdiction of the states. Moreover, the Governor may reserve bills for consideration of the President or intervene in an emergency; or the central Parliament may intervene by two-thirds majority or alter the boundaries of the states.

Unfortunately, in our Constitution, the safeguards required for the unity of a federation, such as an agreement to hold the central Constitution sacrosanct or a part between federal units to surrender authority, have not been included. Consequently, political or other activities can and do encourage separatist tendencies. Moreover, law and others are subjects delegated to the state, thus making the enforcement of any central law depend on the sweet will of the constituent state. Recently, this has become a serious problem—we have the example of a chief minister going on fast and asking people to go on strike, because of the deteriorating law and order situation in the state for which his government would technically be responsible. The central home minister felt that there was deterioration in the law and order situation, while some ministers under the state government disagreed. In Punjab, the state government ministers prepared letters of resignation and forwarded them to the Akali leader, Sant Fateh Singh, to ensure that the state government ministers would not have the responsibility for law and order in the event of the Centre's decision going against the state government on Chandigarh. Again, though CPI(M) leaders in Kerala have stated that they will work under the Constitution, extremist CPI(M) leaders elsewhere have publicly declared themselves against certain features of the Constitution and appeared to have actively supported the breakdown of law and order.

The British, during their rule, ensured that the administrative machinery, particularly the All India Services, strengthened the unity and cohesion of their rule throughout India. At the time of Independence, and for some time thereafter, these services performed a very vital function in continuing that unity and cohesion. But subsequently, they have been steadily denigrated and their unifying role considerably reduced. With the growth of linguistics, the possibility of recruitment of all-India officers through examinations in regional languages, this unifying role will become still be further reduced. Furthermore, with the increase in strength of the states and the increase in the number of linguistic states, the central leadership will depend more and more upon leaders in the states, and their strength in Parliament will depend more and more on the machinery of the state.

The trend of weakening the Centre and strengthening the constituent units would naturally throw a greater burden on the Governor in his coordinating capacity. When I took over governorship in Mysore, the same party was in power in the Centre as in the states, and the responsibilities and duties of the Governor were not clearly defined. Nor, I suppose, was there occasion for it. Largely for this reason, the post of a Governor could be looked upon as a reward for party services, and the post treated almost as a sinecure, like the Duchy of Cornwall. This may have weakened the position of the Governor as a factor in the unifying process. Though I was obviously not appointed as a reward for political services, it seemed unlikely that I could do anything to clarify the positive side of the role of the Governor, unless some opportunity came my way. The only course open to me was the system of weekly letters to the President and the prime minister—not a very positive contribution—as, the prime minister could easily and often did, ignore them.

Owing to the change of governments in a number of states, and the capture of power by parties other than Congress, some considerable discussion has arisen over the role of a Governor, the representative of the president. Recently, in West Bengal, the United Front, which has formed the government, lost some of its supporters, and it was said also the majority in the assembly. It was open to the United Front government to challenge this assertion on the floor of the assembly, but it was then not in session; and the speaker (a nominee of the United Front government) refused to convene the Assembly for some considerable time. Shri Dharma Vira, who was then in the unenviable position of Governor, and who was acceptable to most people in the state, acted as impartially as he could in the circumstances, and dismissed the ministry. The United Front, which came into power again shortly thereafter, however alleged partiality, and contended that he had been appointed without the approval of the chief minister, and he was finally transferred to Mysore.

Discussions in other states, where non-Congress ministries are in power, seem to be leading to the acceptance of the position that a Governor should be acceptable to most parties—that he should act impartially. But in regard to his position, the political discussions have yet to bring out his exact role, in the particular reference to Centre–state relations. If the unity of India is to be a continued goal, presumably his main role will be that of a coordinator.

The Instrument of Instructions, which could have set definite guidance, were not too clear about the validity or legality of the activities contemplated, particularly since these were not adopted by the Constituent Assembly. How was the Governor, for instance, to maintain standards of good administration? How was he himself to promote measures of moral, social and economic welfare, or ensure that all classes took their due share in public life? He could not easily take counsel of the Centre if the government in his state did not belong to the same party, as he was not an agent of the central government.

The activities of coordination appear, however, to be paramount, that is, in obtaining consensus on trickish problems. This is the kind of task so well performed by our last governor general, Lord Mountbatten. He had a thorough understanding of human relationships, and in addition, the charm and persuasiveness to obtain a large measure of consensus on very controversial subjects. He had also considerable administrative experience. Perhaps, this latter ability will also be required in a Governor, who has to take over in the event of an emergency, or a breakdown of the Constitution or of the law and order situation, on behalf of the President.

It seems to me that many people attach a great deal of importance to power. Ours is a democratic republic, and effective power is vested in the people themselves. The power vested in high executives is the power to make fundamental decisions in the nation's activities. A Governor can use his influence to assist his chief minister in selflessly exercising his power for the benefit of the nation. Being a representative of the President, he should also fulfil other necessary functions. He will, for example as chancellor, have direct interest in university education in the state. He is also the recipient of a number of representations in the presentation of which people feel that they have approached the highest office and authority, without affiliation to a group or party. Further, the Governor can advise on questions of policy and measures for promoting the security of the state and the welfare of the people. Finally, he is there in the event of Emergency, to take over administration in the name of the President. The Governor, therefore, has a very important and vital function in the building of the nation's life.

In the changing political scene, the Governor's office can be valuable, because it has considerable bearing on the economic condition of the country. Political changes are inevitable in every country and are often a measure of the flexibility and dynamism of the system, but if the country has to grow economically and develop rapidly, it must inspire in its citizens and in its foreign investors a sense of stability. It has taken most developing countries years to realize that economic stability promotes a sense of security and encourages investment in productive enterprises.

As soon as the sense of insecurity develops, investments in productive enterprises, with the risk involved tend to dry up, and the citizens of the country tend to sink their savings in land, gold and ornaments, which do not contribute adequately to the growth of the country and its economy. It is for the government to encourage investment and divert savings into profitable and useful lines, and this may not easily be accomplished by restrictive measures or by attempting to prevent investment in certain fields. For encouragement to invest, one of the most valuable factors is the sense of stability, which appears to be lacking in the Mao's philosophy. Change may be a very valuable objective, but if the change is through revolution, or at the whims of Red Guards, the climate of development becomes discouraged. Of course, in China, investment by the public is non-existent. In our democracy, it is still an important factor, but its slow decay is placing an impediment in our economy at a time when we have hoped to 'take off'.

In the changing political field, could not the President's representatives in the states (Governors) be useful in promoting the feeling of security? People expect that, though politics and politicians may change, there is always someone outside the normal political hurly-burly who would have a stabilizing influence on the body's economy and politics; and perhaps this is the greatest contribution a Governor can make.

Mysore is a flourishing state with a very promising economic future. It has several modern industries, including an aircraft plant, a telephone industry, a very fine machine-to-tool industry and an electronic complex. The Kolar gold fields are the deepest gold mines in the world, the depth of which it is difficult to imagine until one experiences the enormous heat generated underground. The visitor has to wear thick woollen overalls to prevent a chill when returning to normal surface Mysore temperature, from the heat to which he subjected underground.

Mysore state had some very well-planned cities like Bangalore and Mysore; the beauty of the hills of Coorg, the Jog and other falls; and in addition, the famous Bellur and Halebidu temples. At Bijapur, stands the dominant Gole Gumbaz [sic], the vast Mausoleum of Mohammed Adil Shah, who ruled the kingdom in the seventeenth century. Its magnificent dome is 124 inches in diameter and is the second-largest dome in the world. As only 6 per cent of Mysore state's cultivable land is irrigated, its harvest depends on adequate and timely rains and its food requirements sometimes necessitate an annual import of 3–4 lakh tonnes of rice, largely from Andhra Pradesh. The development activities (the state has vast quantities of high-grade iron ore, manganese and other minerals) had been slowed down for want of power but have accelerated considerably with the recent construction of the mighty Sharavathi projects. The power generated from this project will be utilized not only by large and small industries but also by agriculturists, throughout the main part of the state.

The state has also been known in the past for the spread of education and the efficiency of its administration. It has produced pioneers like Sir M. Visvesvaraya, who engineered the earth dam of the Krishnarajasagar lake, despite the advice of the best western technicians that it was not 'possible'.

Visitors to Mysore are most impressed by Mysore's charm, and they come for such events as the ceremonial Dussehra celebrations, which used to take place once a year; or to see the organization of the exciting Kheda Operations, for capturing wild elephants, which take place as and when additional elephants are required for forest work or for ceremonial occasions. Dussehra celebrations, which mark the end of a ten-day period of gaiety, include a *durbar*, at which the Maharaja's principal officers and families express their assurances of loyalty at this famous Durbar Hall.

Kheda operations are unique and daring. Groups of wild elephants are gradually rounded up, in a process lasting over a month, and finally brought at a pre-fixed date and time into a stockade where they are eventually individually tied and later trained for work. The final part of the Kheda operations presents a spectacular show, which cannot easily be forgotten; the attempts of the wild elephants to escape from the ring of tamed elephants and men, who gradually force them into the stockade; their efforts to break through the stockades, the dependence of the herd on the leader, and the care they take of their young; the final roping of the angry tuskers, and lastly their gradual training into obedient and willing workers. Some tuskers have been so proud and determined that they have died rather than accept captivity.

Incidentally, elephants themselves train their young and discipline their offspring with a judicious use of their trunks.

On 27 May 1964, while was touring the state, I received the tragic news of death of our beloved prime minister, Shri Jawaharlal Nehru. He was the most illustrious man of his age, and it was difficult to think of India without him. His death was also a great personal loss, for I had been working in close touch with him for the last eighteen years.

The Indo–Pakistan war broke out in 1965, by which time I had relinquished charge of the governorship of Mysore to Shri V.V. Giri and had completely retired.

Epilogue

I have been fortunate in having had varied administrative experiences. I have held leadership posts in the armed forces, civil administration and a training institution geared around business management; and I have realized that in each set-up, the administration has its own peculiar problems and its own contribution to make, whether it is military administration, industrial management, research administration or civil administration; in the secretariat or in the field. Having been in touch with all these facets of administration, I believe that there are several lessons to be learnt. But in setting down some experiences, or in attempting to present some thoughts on the various aspects of administration, I am reminded of a much-repeated story of a very important person, returning by plane from a successful tour abroad.

As the plane was circling over his hometown, he drew out a Rs 100-note and asked the air hostess to drop it from the plane, so that at least the person who would find it would be pleased because of his return. One of the passengers who heard him giving these instructions, suggested that instead of dropping a single Rs 100-note, he might consider dropping ten notes, each of Rs 10 denomination, so that ten people instead of one, would be happy that the VIP had returned. Another passenger suggested that the VIP might go a step further and drop a hundred notes, each of Re 1 denomination, so that a hundred people would be pleased instead of only ten; for ten was, after all, a very small percentage in a population of 40 lakh. A thoughtful-looking passenger, who had been silently listening to these remarks, suggested that, instead of dropping currency notes, a better solution might be, for the VIP to throw himself out of the plane because that would satisfy everybody. Satisfying a large number of people has become necessary in the new India, which has accepted democracy and is trying to build up a welfare state. The government is also trying to eliminate the basis on which communism has been built in other countries. But India can still go communist if our five-year plans fail, or the pressure of population becomes intolerable and prices continue to rise. It is difficult to foresee what India of tomorrow will be. One thing is certain. It will be different from the India of today. So, we have no alternative but to train our young men and women to prepare themselves to meet these challenges, where privilege is no longer inherited and all people are equal.

Referring back to administration I have been wondering as India has built up a great deal of experience (both good and bad) of administration in these twenty-three years of Independence, whether we could not build up an effective administrative system of our own, making use of the good experience, and eschewing as necessary, the bad. I am convinced also that the military system can learn a great deal from the civil and equally the civil administration from the military.

For example, the armed forces lay great emphasis on two vital aspects:

(1) Training

In the armed forces, a man, or an officer is learning throughout his career, undergoing training, attending courses and taking tests, and he is familiarizing himself all the time with new equipment, new arms and new systems. It has again and again been proved in war that the army, which has habituated itself with its weapons and its terrain and its tactics, will destroy an enemy which has failed to train its troops. This experience has been brought home to us in two wars—our debacle against the Chinese, where our troops were asked to fight at unaccustomed heights, unacclimatized to the weather or the terrain, and our success against the superior weapons and armour of Pakistan, through intensive training and familiarization with our own weapons. We have forgotten that (Field Marshal Erwin) Rommel trained his Afrika Corps to be accustomed to fighting with tanks in excessive heat, prior to taking them into the desert battle. We have equally forgotten that Israelis are likely to prove more than a match for Arab troops, as long as they continue to train more intensively and in a more coordinated manner than the neighbouring Arab countries.

For some reasons which I have not been able to fathom, the civil service do not appear to believe in training. The success of the Indian Civil Service under the British may have led them to believe that they could turn their hands to new tasks with equal vigour and without training. But this did not apply to every member of that august service. George Abell (now Sir George) was triple blue and a double first and played his best cricket when he had not practiced, but he was an exception. And we forget that the British were constantly personally training their subordinates 'on the job'.

Some of our big businessmen at one time thought that it was only necessary to be born into the family or carry into the family, to be equally successful in business. But these ideas are rapidly changing; and more and mere scions of these families are now 'management trained'. However, large portions of the civil services, the forest, the police, the postal services, are still trained on the job. Training 'on the job' is a wonderful method of training, provided, however, we can afford the time and the wastage. I do not believe we have that time or the necessary skilled personnel at our disposal to depend only on 'on the job' training.

(2) Discipline

Somehow, this concept is treated as purely of interest to the armed forces. Whereas, to me, a soldier, it appears, that discipline is the core of the essential concomitants of economic development. It was discipline and hard work that turned Germany from total destruction to the most flourishing economy of Europe. It was discipline that turned a poor, backward country into the powerful nation of Japan and resurrected it after its defeat into a country with the highest rate of growth; and it was discipline that changed the economics of Pakistan from a depressed state to one of fast growth. Of course, it is not discipline alone; but, perhaps, I should say that discipline is a very necessary concomitant even for our liberal democracy.

Our democracy could be tempered with enough discipline to help our economy take better shape. The civil services can and have taught us a great deal, though they are not at their best in the present conditions, when they have been successively denigrated and demoralized. We are apt to forget that they virtually ran the administration and oiled the wheels of government during the period immediately after the Partition and accepted responsibilities which would have broken tougher shoulders. During that period, they were models for us to follow and to envy, and we did envy them—their efficiency, their power and their status. But the effort to denigrate the civil service has turned the machine into a bureaucracy of red tape and caused us a great deal of harm, and in that effort, we have lost a valuable legacy.

We may have the most representative and most vocal Parliaments, which may enact excellent law, but these laws will be of little value to us if we have not the administrative machine for their execution after enactment. We shall degenerate into the Japan of Gilbert's fame when the Mikado's orders were so revered that they were treated as infallible. But being so infallible, no one bothered to carry them out. However, when the civil services were functioning as an efficient machine, they gave us the experience of precise thought and expression, of well-calculated and thought-out plans, of precise delegation; and of the acceptance of responsibility at all levels—all necessary for efficient administration.

Lately, we have gained a great deal from the experiences of industrial and business management—the scientific approach, the method and improvements and techniques connected therewith, the techniques of planning, execution and control, and the need for the understanding of group psychology.

Administrative Staff College taught me how wide can the differences be in experiences of different individuals, and how much can be gained from such experiences if properly integrated. Surely, we could, with all the vast administrative experiences through which we have accumulated, integrate them into an administrative system for training our future administrators. Should it not be almost a duty for those in India who have been through such experiences to set them down to promote a 'dialogue'. In our country, which has to nurse its resources, we cannot afford the different systems of administration, which have grown up in the various spheres of activity. But we can make use of those systems to build up an administration tailored specially to suit our requirements.

Some years ago, my eldest son Satish had graduated from the Indian Military Academy, Dehradun, and was

commissioned as a 2nd Lieutenant in the 2nd Maratha
Light Infantry (Kali Panchwin). At the academy, he had
won the 'Sword of Honour' but was prevented from
personally receiving this award by an unfortunate riding
accident the evening before the passing out parade. After
he had recovered, he was posted to his battalion, where
after a few years' service, he was selected as adjutant. His
subsequent career was also very successful. Therefore,
I was sorry to hear from him that he wished to leave the
army because he thought that the army no longer provided
an attractive career. I wrote to him as follows:

*You feel that the army career today is not as attractive
for young men of our country, as it was previously. This
is probably so. But perhaps no office in the country today
is as glamorous as it was say, thirty years ago. Times
have changed and the accent is on money. Glamour then
surrounded army officers, but it was of a superficial kind.
At the same time, in the regiment and the Mess, Indians
were not treated as equals. Indian food was seldom served
in the Mess and listening to Indian music was invariably
discouraged. In fact, everything Indian was frowned upon.
Further, the belief was nurtured and spread that Indian
Officers were not capable of providing a high standard of
leadership. Operations on the North-West Frontier and in
the Second World War, where Indian officers successfully*

led troops into battle, soon dispelled this myth. It was unfortunate also that, at that time, several responsible people in public life in our country gave our young men no encouragement at all for entering this noble service.

I believe there is as great a future for young men joining the army today, as there was some years ago. There is of course greater competition, because of the larger numbers, coming into the army, a necessary feature in every walk of life in the country, if merit is to succeed.

You must remember that today you are rebuilding an army on nationalistic lines, and in a democratic way, in effect our own army. There are contrary communal and linguistic pulls; but I believe, the armed forces will in time counteract such pulls. Further, you are representing the core of a truly national service in the defence of our country. Surely no services or association in India provides a greater measure of unity or a finer example of nationalism than the armed forces.

You have suggested that the administrative or the foreign service would offer you a better career. Even if it were now possible for you to change your service, are the civil services, really what you require? You have demonstrated your special interest in subjects pertaining to the military profession, such as tactics, military history, military administration and man management. Interest in the work a man does is the greatest single factor in human happiness. If then, the right kind of work gives a man so much emotional satisfaction, the career he chooses must be to his liking. You have proved to yourself that you like work in the army, and the Army has shown you, that it likes you.

Do you think that you will get the same satisfaction from the foreign service or the administrative service? There used to be a great deal of glamour in the foreign service, but with the expansion of communications, most of that glamour has gone. The number of officers frustrated in that service has now alarmingly increased.

You have also written about shortage of finances. You have to understand that the value of the rupee, being what it is, all of us who were working for a living thirty years ago and are still working for a living today, have always been short of money. We have no alternative but to exercise strict control over our expenditure.

I would also like to say to you that there is in the army, a challenge not only in meeting aggression but also in building up a disciplined national corps, devoted to the country, built up on hard work and developing that leadership which you appear to have in you.

It will be worth your while to ponder over these few thoughts and not lose the interest you have in the army. You know that a horse will burst into a gallop when spurred. A mind is like that also. So, Satish, put spurs into

*it and move on at a smart pace, ignoring people who ask
you, apparently, innocently, 'Why did you join the army?'
Tell them that if you had chosen banking or accountancy,
would they have asked you a similar question? What these
people should now say to you is, 'Congratulations Satish,
on joining the army, for only men with courage and a sense
of patriotism join the armed forces. I believe that a time
will come when the majority of our countrymen will also
be saying this.'*

I heard later from Satish that he was not fully convinced.

I have wondered again what induces a young man
to select a certain profession? His parents or relations.
Satish's uncle J.M. thought he was a born leader and
would go a very long way in the armed forces, where he
had already done so well. His father and mother had given
their advice. But the choice was his. In the past, the prestige
of the government service, or the glamour of the armed
forces had drawn some of our young men. But prestige
and glamour were perhaps to be denigrated in a socialistic
society—at least they did not seem to exert the same
influence now. The best of our young men was turning,
not to the professions, but to business enterprises where
the prospects of the very much larger emoluments seemed
to be a positive lure. Some of the business houses had also
drawn off the best talent by offering excellent conditions
of service, which the armed forces and the government

services could not afford to emulate. Of course, there was the intense desire, which we all seemed to have, of wanting to serve the country in some way and hope to take part in its development. But that desire does not seem to be so intense amongst younger men today. Perhaps, this is because of their disappointment with our political, economic and developmental accomplishments. Surely it is now time to think of encouraging young men to join the services, particularly the armed forces?

The cause of this revulsion feeling, almost universal, against the 'establishment' seems partly due to the failure of earlier generations to establish a society conforming to the ideas and ideas of the younger generations. In the west, this disappointment with the establishment had partly been the outcome of two disastrous wars, and the development of a society whose main God appears to be money. But what are the reasons for such feelings in India? Is our society orienting its values around money and wealth? And what has happened to the traditional values of our glorious civilization of self-denial, of sacrifice and of sacrifice and of the higher spiritual values? Are they to have no influence whatsoever on our future? At a time when the west is turning more and more to obtaining lessons from our culture? Perhaps, however, in attempting to find political solutions for our various problems, these traditional values must die.

The best years of my life have been devoted to this magnificent profession of arms. I firmly believe that our young men will do well in choosing the services as their career. They will have much work ahead of them, for their task will always be to keep abreast with fast moving developments, for the fate of those who one day will be under their command, will hang upon their knowledge, acquired by industry and earnestness. But, as it is often said industry and earnestness will be valueless, unless they are consecrated by the resolution to be in all things 'Men of Honour' and 'Men of Integrity', not as understood in the usual sense only, but in the highest; for honour and integrity are greater than fame.

Looking back, my thoughts often turn to the large family of soldiers to which I belong and also to other service personnel, who had been my companions throughout my service. They are my companions in retirement also, for now we are ex-servicemen, belonging to an association (the Indian Ex-Servicemen League) which exists for the sole purpose of looking after ex-servicemen's welfare and granting financial aid to them and their dependants. Like other similar organizations, the stability and achievements of this association rest, apart from other things, on a steady flow of donations through public support. Today this support is lacking, and the largest donations come from the UK. I feel that this is due to a lack of knowledge and not because of disrespect for the soldier. Our soldiers' heroism in the Indo-Pak conflict, the China war, and the Kashmir war of 1947–48 has been understood and appreciated. But our people have yet to be educated to the fact that the ex-servicemen's welfare is a deserving cause; not only to honour those to whom honour is due, but also to give an incentive to future recruitment. I am reminded of an inscription I saw on a war memorial at Kohima in Nagaland, which reads:

'When you go home
Tell them of us, and say,
For their tomorrow
We gave our today.'

Acknowledgements

I could not conclude this narrative without acknowledging my great debt to my brother J.M., who has assisted me since the inception of this task and helped me to recast and rewrite certain chapters.

To my wife, who has encouraged me to embark on this task and to persevere in it.

To Mr Justice Sharma who, at Chandigarh, has read through the manuscripts and made certain comments.

And to a host of others who have periodically commented upon the preliminary drafts.

Glossary

ADC: Aide-de-camp—a military officer acting as a confidential assistant to a senior officer.

Bde: Bde stands for Brigade. A brigade typically consists of several battalions and is commanded by a brigadier.

- Division: Composed of 3–4 brigades.
- Brigade: Composed of several battalions.
- Battalion: Composed of several companies.
- Company: Composed of several platoons.

Bn: 'Bn' in context of the Indian Army stands for battalion. A battalion (Bn) is an operational unit in the military, consisting of around 800 to 1200 soldiers, commanded by a lieutenant colonel and is made up smaller sub-units ('companies'). Each company is commanded by a major or captain.

There are different types of battalions in the Indian Army, including:

- Infantry Battalion: Composed of soldiers trained in ground combat and infantry tactics.
- Artillery Battalion: Specialized in operating heavy weapons like guns, howitzers and mortars.
- Armoured Battalion: Includes tanks and armoured vehicles for mechanized warfare.
- Engineers Battalion: Responsible for engineering tasks such as constructing bridges, fortifications and mine clearance.
- Signal Battalion: Handles communication and signal operations.

Brig.: Abbreviation for brigadier (see **Bde**).

C. Regt: An infantry regiment formed by the British during the Second World War to increase the strength of the Indian Army. The regiment was formed along caste lines and fought against the Japanese in Burma. It was disbanded in 1946.

C-in-C: C-in-C stands for Commander-in-Chief of the Indian Army. Before the restructuring of India's military command structure in 1955, the Commander-in-Chief was the highest-ranking officer in the Indian Army, who was responsible for its strategic direction and operational leadership. The term C-in-C is no longer used in official contexts to refer to the head of the army, but it may occasionally appear in historical or ceremonial discussions.

Chief of the Army Staff (COAS): On 1 April 1955, the title of Commander-in-Chief was officially changed to Chief of the Army Staff (COAS). It remains the position of highest authority in the Indian Army today.

DSO: Distinguished Service Order—military decoration of the United Kingdom, as well as formerly of other parts of the Commonwealth, awarded for operational gallantry for highly successful command and leadership during active operations, typically in actual combat.

EWT: Exercise With Troops—a military exercise conducted by the Integrated Battle Group (IBG). The IBG is a plan to change the course of war by having infantry, armoured and artillery troops train and fight together.

Flt Lt: Flight Lieutenant is a commissioned officer rank in the Indian Air Force (IAF) that is equivalent to a captain in the army and a lieutenant in the navy.

GOC-in-C: General Officer Commanding-in-Chief—a military rank that is given to a general officer who commands a large or important command. GOC-in-Cs are usually one rank higher than a GOC, and GOCs of corps-level formations report to them.

HEH: His Excellency Highness—'His Excellency' is a third-person form of address used to refer to heads of state and government in republican countries. Highness is a royal address. For royal heads, such as the Nizam of Hyderabad, His Excellency Highness was used.

IAF: Indian Air Force.

INA: Indian National Army—a military force that fought against the British during the Second World War.

ICOs: ICOs refer to Indian Military Academy (IMA) cadets who are selected to become Indian Commissioned Officers. The term ICO can also colloquially refer to the officer cadre itself and any individual who is commissioned as an officer is an Indian Commissioned Officer. They are distinguished from Junior Commissioned Officers (JCOs) and Non-Commissioned Officers (NCOs), both of whom have different ranks and responsibilities.

ICS: Indian Civil Service—officially known as the Imperial Civil Service, was the higher civil service of the British Empire in India during British rule.

IDSM: Indian Distinguished Service Medal—a former military decoration awarded to Indian citizens in the British Empire's armed forces and military police for distinguished service.

IEME: The India Army Corps of Electronics and Mechanical Engineers (IEME) is an arms and service branch of the Indian Army. The Corps has varying responsibilities related to the design, development, trial, inspection and refit of weapon systems and equipment. They also provide technical advice to units and conduct recovery operations in peace and war.

IMS: Indian Medical Service—a former military medical service in British India that also had some civilian functions. It was in existence until India gained independence in 1947.

JCOs: Junior Commissioned Officers, or JCOs, are individuals who hold a commission but are still considered part of the enlisted ranks, typically at a senior level (e.g., Subedar, Subedar Major).

KCIOs: Kings Commissioned Indian Officers, abbreviated as KCIOs, were Indian officers who were granted commissions in the British Army under the authority of the British monarch before India gained Independence in 1947. They held ranks equivalent to British officers and were trained at the Royal Military Academy of Sandhurst in the UK and the Indian Military Academy (IMA) in Dehradun. After India's Independence, these officers continued to serve in the Indian Army which transitioned into the independent armed forces of India. The term is historically significant as it when Indians began to hold leadership positions which were held by British officers.

MC: Military Cross—a military decoration awarded to members of the British Armed Forces for gallantry in combat.

MBE: Member of the Order of the British empire—a British honour given to people who have made significant contributions to society.

Mikado: Japanese term for emperor.

Naga Underground: Phizo created an underground government called the Naga Federal Government (NFG) and a Naga Federal Army (NFA).

NEFA: North-East Frontier Agency—a political division in British India and the Republic of India until 1972. It was the name of the area that is now the state of Arunachal Pradesh.

NWFP: North-West Frontier Province—a province of British India, the Dominion of Pakistan and the Islamic Republic of Pakistan.

OTC: Officer Training Corps in India provides training to young men and women who are studying in universities or colleges. The training is designed to prepare them for a potential career in the Indian Army as officers. It offers an opportunity to serve in the armed forces without a full-time commitment immediately.

ORS: ORS stands for Other Ranks of enlisted personnel who are not commissioned officers. It is used to collectively describe the soldiers, non-commissioned officers (NCOs) and junior commissioned officers (JCOs).

- Enlisted Personnel: These are the soldiers who serve as soldiers, technicians, clerks and in various other roles.
- Non-Commissioned Officers (NCOs): These are senior enlisted personnel who have earned promotions and have leadership responsibilities (e.g., Havildar, Naik).

RMC: Royal Military College—known as the Royal Military Academy Sandhurst today, this institute was formed on the site of the former Royal Military College (founded in 1801 for the training of officers for arms other than the Royal Artillery and Royal Engineers) in 1947 when it amalgamated with the Royal Military Academy in Woolwich (founded in 1741 for the training of officers for the Royal Artillery and Royal Engineers).

Tpt Sqn: Transport Squadron—a squadron of the British Army, such as the 20 Transport Squadron Royal Logistic Corps or the 216 Tpt Sqn RLC EPLS Sect Comd.

Triple blue and a double first: Academic distinctions awarded at Cambridge and Oxford universities.

VC: Victoria Cross—Britain's highest award for gallantry and is given to those who display extraordinary bravery, self-sacrifice or devotion to duty in the face of the enemy.

General Shrinagesh, a pioneering leader of
independent India's military

Scan QR code to access the
Penguin Random House India website